Practical Travel

Provence

(France)

1992

Hayit Publishing

[1st] Edition 1992
UK Edition: ISBN 1 874251 40 1
US Edition: ISBN 1 56634 002 0

Authors: Carola Manstein-Blechinger, Nicolai Blechinger
Translation, Adaption, Revision: Scott Reznik
Print: Schroff Druck, Augsburg/Germany
Photography: Carola Manstein-Blechinger, Nicolai Blechinger,
French Office of Tourism
Maps: Ralf Tito

 Printed in Germany

THE PROVENCE
Vaison-la-Romaine
ORANGE
ALÈS
CARPENTRAS
Sorgues
AVIGNON
NÎMES
Cereste
Pertuis
St.-Gilles
ARLES
SALON-DE-PR.
Miramas
AIX-EN-PROVENCE
La Grde.-Motte
Camargue
Etang de
Vaccarès
Etang de Berre
S^{tes} Maries-de-la-Mer
MARTIGUES
Gulf of Lyon
MARSEILLE
0
km
12
N

Using this Book

Books in the *Practical Travel* series offer a wealth of practical information. You will find the most important tips for your travels conveniently arranged in alphabetical order. Cross-references aid in orientation so that even entries which are not covered in depth, for instance "Holiday Apartments," lead you to the appropriate entry, in this case "Accommodation." Also thematically altered entries are also cross-referenced. For example under the heading "Medication," there appear the following references: "Medical Care," "Pharmacies," "Vaccinations."

With travel guides from the *Practical Travel* series the information is already available before you depart on your trip. Thus, you are already familiar with necessary travel documents and maps, even customs regulations. Travel within the country is made easier through comprehensive presentation of public transportation, car rentals in addition to the practical tips ranging from medical assistance to newspapers available in the country. The descriptions of cities are arranged alphabetically as well and include the most important facts about the particular city, its history and a summary of significant sights. In addition, these entries include a wealth of practical tips — from shopping, restaurants and accommodation to important local addresses. Background information does not come up short either. You will find interesting information about the people and their culture as well as the regional geography, history and current political and economic situation.

As a particular service to our readers, *Practical Travel* includes prices in hard currencies so that they might gain a more accurate impression of prices even in countries with high rates of inflation. Most prices quoted in this book have been converted to US$ and £.

Contents

Registry of Places

General Information

Accommodation

An octagonal blue sign on hotels offers information on the category, into which all French hotels are grouped. The year quoted on the sign is the date of the last inspection and resulting classification. The number of stars has nothing to do with the Michelin Guide, which only judges the quality of cuisine.

****L first-class luxury hotels

**** luxury hotels

*** very comfortable hotels

** comfortable hotels

* moderately comfortable hotels

Logis de France (LF) = typically Provençal hotels offering regional cuisine, usually located outside of the towns and sometimes housed in splendid villas or châteaus (these can be recognised by a green sign with a yellow fireplace).

Gîte d'Etape, Gîte rural/Gîtes ruraux = holiday on a farm (ferme).

Hôtel garni = offers accommodation only sometimes including breakfast.

In the Département Vaucluse alone there are about 47 Logis de France, 600 Gîte d'Etape, 5,000 hotel rooms, four youth hostels and 96 camping areas (with 20,700 sites). In the low season, one can usually count on a discount between 10 and 15%, especially if the room is booked for a number of days. (The camping areas will usually give a discount of 20%.) In addition to this, there is a large selection of private lodging. The hotels and restaurants listed in this guide constitutes only a selection of those available and by no means do they infer recommendation. Those who would like hotel recommendations should consult the updated "Michelin" guide, which is based on constant review of the hotels.

Aigues-Mortes →*Camargue*

Aix-en-Provence

Population: about 124,000; elevation: 175 metres (573 feet)

Aix-en-Provence, once the capital of the Provence, is a bustling university city with an aristocratic atmosphere. Expansive palaces, boulevards and countless squares with fountains make for a wonderful stroll through the city.

Aix-en-Provence / **History**

After the Romans completely destroyed the Gaelic sanctum of "Entrement" in 123 B.C., the Gauls founded the city of Aquae Sextiae about 2 km (1¼ miles) away. This city was first developed by the Romans as a base for their battles,

AIX-EN-PROVENCE OLD TOWN

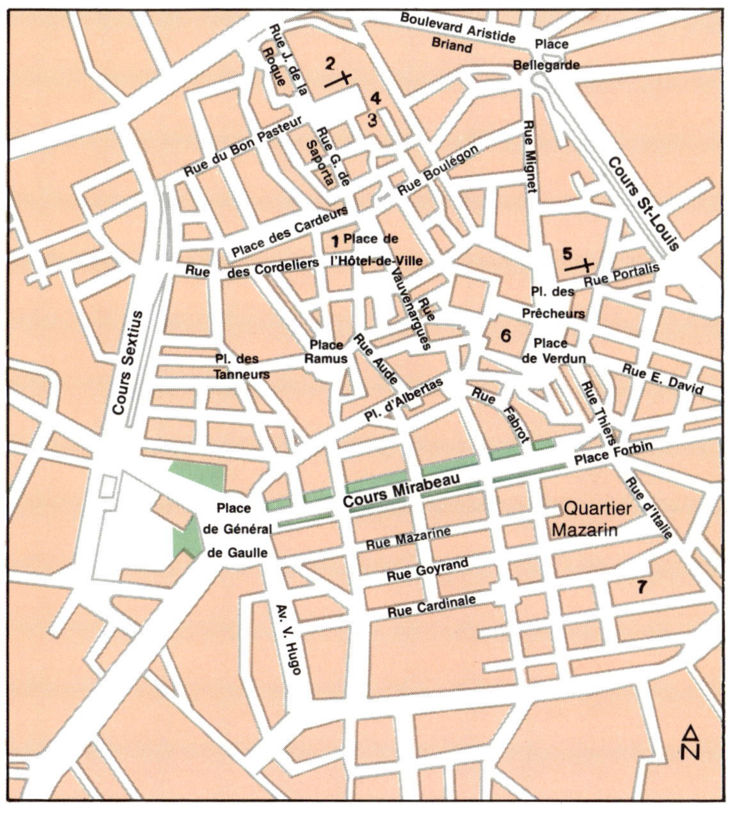

Legend:

1. Hôtel de Ville
2. St-Sauveur
3. Palais archiépiscopal
4. Musée de Tapisserie
5. St-Madeleine
6. Palais de Justice
7. Musée Granet

and a number of the Roman buildings were constructed by the general Gaius Marius. During the reign of Augustus, the city was renamed Colonia Julia Augusta Aquis Sextis and was made the administration centre for the region. It was of importance to the city that the road "Via Aurelia," transversing the country, passed directly through town. Aix was temporarily the capital city of the Province Gallia Narbonensis Secunda. The city maintained its significance into the 4th century; from that point on, its importance waned. Aix was the residence of the Counts of the Provence (1246-1484). Under King René from the house of Anjou (1409-1480), the city was expanded, becoming an economic and commercial centre. "Good King René," as he was called by the people, attracted not only many artists through his patronage, but was simultaneously concerned with the economy. For example, he introduced the muscatel grape and the mulberry tree used in breeding silkworms. Aix experienced a high point in its history. The parliament, appointed by the French king around 1500, gained power and influence. This standing parliament, relatively autonomous and consisting of noblemen, was a court of law which increasingly pursued the goal of the independence of the Provence from the French kingdom. The special rights and privileges strengthened the confidence of the middle class, reflected by the buildings inside the city. Up until the French Revolution in 1789, Aix held a position of economic and political power. Thereafter, Marseille began to take over this preeminent role. Today, tourism, the university and museums help in increasing the significance of Aix.

Aix-en-Provence / **Sights**

The old part of Aix is enclosed by a ring of boulevards and avenues running parallel to the former city fortifications. The Cours Mirabeau begins on Place Général-de-Gaulle with its impressive fountains from 1860. To the north is the old city, the former bourgeois quarter extending to the Bishops' Quarter. To the south, the Quartier Mazarin laid out in 1646 also contains a number of beautiful palaces and fountains. Further to the south and to the west is the modern portion of Aix, symbolised by the Fondation Vasarely.

A good place to begin a walking tour of the city is at the Cours Mirabeau, the grandiose boulevard with its massive, shady plane trees and no less than three fountains. Along this boulevard there seems to be one palais after the other. In addition, there are a number of interesting shops, bookstores, numerous cafés and restaurants. North of the boulevard on Rue Espariat in the Hôtel Boyer d'Eguilles from 1675 is the Muséon d'Histoire naturelle (Museum of Natural History — closed Sundays and Holidays). The museum is not only famous for its Provençal fossils and minerals, but also for its collection of fossilised dinosaur eggs, originating from the archaeological find on the southern St-Victoire slopes. After crossing the Place d'Albertas and Place St-Honoré with their fountains, then passing the Palace of Justice, one will come upon the Ste-Marie-Madeleine Church. Incorporating Gothic remains from the 13th century, this church was constructed in the 17th century. In the middle of the 19th century, it was given a new Baroque façade. Back in the alleyways of the old city, a street leads to the Place de l'Hôtel-de-Ville, the city hall square. Located on this square (the flower market also takes place here) are the post office and municipal administration, housed in the Halle aux Grains, an old grain storage facility with gables decorated with sculptures from the 18th century. The city hall was built in Baroque architecture in the 17th century and has splendid wrought-iron gates. This building also houses the famous book collection of Marquis de Méjanes (1726-1786; earlier, the Consul of Aix), totalling 30,000 editions. In this building is also the St-John Perse foundation, named after the French diplomat and poet (1887-1975), who was awarded the Nobel Prize for Literature in 1960. Built in the 16th century, the Tour de l'Horloge (clock tower) adjacent to the city hall has a typically Proveçale Barbarotte (bell cage) and used to be a watch tower. Continuing north, one will come upon the Musée du Vieil Aix. This regional museum contains, among other exhibits, a collection of Santon figures and marionettes, which once made up the "speaking" nativity scenes. Before visiting the Cathedral St-Sauveur, one should visit the Musée des Tapisseries. In this building, formerly a aristocratic bishop's palace from the 17th century, tapestries hang on the walls. These are witness of the times in which only the wealthy could afford to decorate their homes with the lavish weavings. Wedged into the pattern of alleyways in the old city, the famous Cathedral St-Sauveur towers above the rooftops. This cathedral unites the entire spectrum of architectural styles, from the early Romanesque to the late Renaissance. Originating from a Roman temple wall on the old Via Aurelia, the cathedral was built from the 5th to the 17th century. Inside, the baptistery from the 5th century is especially worth seeing as is the famous triptychon of the burning bush from the 15th century. It depicts King René and Queen Jeanne kneeling before Mary and the Christ Child. For a small gratuity, the church attendant will be happy to open the protective wooden shutters. Through a side door, one can get to the cloître (cloister).

About 1 km (about ½ mile) heading out of town one will come to the Cézanne Atelier. Paul Cézanne (1839-1906) spent his last years in this house. His studio on the second floor has been preserved as he left it (open from 10 am to noon and 2 to 6 pm, closing one hour earlier during the off-season; closed Tuesdays and Fridays).

The Fondation Vasarely is located on the western outskirts of town on a knoll. This is the second monument to have been erected in France by the Hungarian artist Victor Vasarely *(→Gordes).* This massive complex of buildings is certainly controversial, made of aluminium, glass and cement and leaving a surrealistic impression. The foundation (open Wednesday to Monday from 9:30 am to 12:30 pm and 2 to 5:30 pm) contains a studies centre in addition to tapestries and geometric paintings. Vasarely's kinetic art is presented on the second floor.

Northwest of the old city, where the Roman baths Thermes Sextius were located earlier, is now the location of a therapeutic spa from the 18th century. Patients with circulatory problems are treated in the therapeutic baths with a water temperature of 34 °C (94 °F). Ruins from Roman country villas have been excavated here as well. In the park adjacent to the spa, a watch tower still stands. This was once a part of the fortification wall built in the 14th century.

→Vauvenargues (Picasso)

Aix-en-Provence / **Practical Information**

Accommodation

Hotels: **** Paul Cézanne (without restaurant), modern accommodation, 40 avenue Victor-Hugo, Tel: (42) 26 34 73, 44 rooms 490-1000 FF.

*** Pullman Le Pigonnet (beautiful location within a park), 5 avenue Pigonnet, Tel: (42) 59 02 90, 50 rooms 350-750 FF, restaurant serving complete meals priced up to 250 FF

** Caravelle (without restaurant), 29 boulevard Roi René, Tel: (42) 21 53 05, 30 rooms 170-280 FF.

** Le Moulin (without restaurant), modern accommodation, 1 avenue Schumann, Tel: (42) 59 41 68, 37 rooms 150-280 FF.

* Cardinal (without restaurant), 24 rue Cardinale, Tel: (42) 38 32 30, 23 rooms 130-300 FF.

Camping: Chantecler, to the east of town, Tel: (42) 26 12 98.

Arc en Ciel, Pont des 3-Sautets, south of town, Tel: (42) 26 14 28.

Automobile Repairs: Alfa-Romeo, BMW, Ford, Honda, Mercedes-Benz, Peugeot-Talbot, Renault, Toyota, Volkswagen, Volvo.

Entertainment: Aix is internationally renowned for its music festivals in July and August. Concerts, theatre and dance performances, chansons and jazz make for a rich selection of cultural activities. A calendar of events is available through the Office de Tourisme.

Medical Care: On-call medical service, Tel: (42) 26 04 81.

Hospital: Centre Hospitalier, avenue de Tamaris, Tel: (42) 23 98 00.

Restaurants: *** Clos de Violette (Banzo), especially worth recommending for its specialities, 10 avenue Violette, Tel: (42) 23 30 71, reservations are recommended, complete meals 250-350 FF.

** Abbaye des Cordeliers, 21 rue Lieutaud, Tel: (42) 27 29 47, complete meals 95-158 FF.

Shopping: The flower market takes place in front of the city hall on Tuesdays, Thursdays and Saturdays; the flea market is at the Palace of Justice and the weekly market, at Place des Prêcheurs in front of the Ste-Marie-Madeleine Church.

Sports Facilities: The golf course d'Aix-Marseille is located about 8.5 km (5½ miles) west of town on the D 9, Tel: (42) 24 20 41.

Transportation: In Aix, it is a good idea to explore the city on foot or use the buses. This is especially true in the inner city, which is in part, a pedestrian zone. Aix is a hub for rail travel and is therefore easily accessible by train.

Important Addresses: Office de Tourisme, place Général-de-Gaulle, Tel: (42) 26 02 93.

Alpilles

South of St-Rémy, a 300-400 metre (980-1,310 foot) high range of limestone mountains. Its white, rugged cliffs shimmer in the sunlight. The range is covered sparsely with a few oaks and pines among the maquis. One is able to hike along the marked path for up to five hours. For cyclists, there are also a number of bike paths varying in degree of difficulty. One can fish in the five acre lake for trout and other whitefish. The tourist office in St-Rémy can provide more detailed information as well as hiking and cycling maps.

Ansouis

Population: approximately 650

Ansouis lies 8 km (5 miles) north of Pertuis on the D 56 and is a small town on a rock formation with a famous castle.

Built in the 10th century, the castle is still partially inhabited by the descendants of the founder, the Duke of Sabran. The castle can be toured daily from 2:30 to 6 pm (closed Tuesdays). A well known park also belongs to the castle. The Musée Extraordinaire, furnished with Provençal furnishings and housed in a building from the 14th century, exhibits finds from the underwater world of the scuba diver Georges Mazoyer: coral, shells and Luberon fossils.

Apt

Population: about 12,000; elevation: 230 metres (752 feet)
Apt lies on the N 100 in th Calavon Valley, approximately 55 km (35 miles) east of Avignon and 54 km (34 miles) northeast of Aix-en-Provence.

Apt / **History**

The city of Apta Julia was founded by the Romans around 38 B.C. on the Via Domitia, the roadway leading from Italy and the Rhône Valley. Over the years, the city became the capital of the Provence. The Pont Julien bridge *(→Julien Bridge),* located a few miles outside of town, is exemplary of these times. The bridge is in excellent condition and is still used today. During the 3rd century, Apt was the seat of the bishop and construction in Apt would continue to flourish during the Middle Ages (see St. Annen Cathedral). In recent times, the city has become a centre for the production of ochre, mined in the nearby region of Roussillon. The significance of ochre mining has slackened due to the discovery of synthetic substitutes. Ochre is only used today primarily in house paint. However, Apt maintained its significance in its world-wide renown for the production of candied fruit and jams.

Apt / **Sights**

After following the main road N 100 past the less aesthetic industrial area, one will enter the lovely small city of Apt with its numerous points of interest. Across the Place de la Bouquerie with its many pleasant cafés and through the lively shopping streets, one will come upon the St-Annen Cathedral. The building was originally founded during the rule of the Merovingians as a basilica. It was destroyed in the 11th century and subsequently rebuilt. The cathedral was then continually expanded during the 13th as well as the 16th and 17th centuries, offering visitors a collage of different architectural styles. Worth seeing inside are paintings from the Middle Ages, a Roman altar and two impressive crypts, one above the other. The lower crypt is presumed to originate from the Merovingian period, while the upper exhibits Roman elements. The cathedral is open daily with the exception of Saturday and Sunday afternoons as well as Mondays. Not far from the cathedral on the Rue de l'Amphithéâtre, the Archaeological Museum, housed in the municipal palace from the 18th century, displays a collection of Fayences (glazed earthenware) in addition to a large variety of finds from the Roman time period. The museum is open from 10 am to noon and from 2:30 to 5:30 pm (during the off-season, until 4:30 pm). The museum is closed Tuesdays, Sundays, holidays and Saturday afternoons. If at all possible, one should visit the traditional market in Apt on Saturday between 8 am and noon. Everything is sold here, including fresh fruit, vegetables and fish, olives in every variety, goat's cheese, household goods, baskets woven locally, live chickens, flowers, fabrics and articles of clothing as well as every kind of souvenir.

Apt / **Practical Information**

Accommodation

Hotels: *** Auberge du Luberon, 17 quai Léon-Sagy, Tel: (90) 74 12 50, 16 rooms priced from 190 to 450 FF, meals from 130 to 360 FF.

** Aptois (without restaurant), 6 cours Lauze-de-Perret, Tel: (90) 74 02 02, 26 rooms, 100-200 FF.

In nearby Gargas: Chambre d'Hôte and Table d'Hôte/Gîte de France Moulin de Lavon, Yves Nief, route de Perrotet, Tel: (90) 74 34 54.

Camping: ** Camping municipal Les Cèdres, Routes de Rustrel (150 sites), Tel: (90) 74 14 61.

Camping-Caravaning Le Luberon, route de Saignon (150 sites), Tel: (90) 74 23 93.

Automobile Repairs: Citroën, Ford, Peugeot-Talbot.

Entertainment: In addition to two cinemas (César and Palace) and a theatre, there are numerous festivals and other cultural activities. Further information can be obtained at the Tourist Information Office.

Medical Care: Apt offers very good medical care for both general and specialised medicine. Hospital, route de Marseille, Tel: (90) 74 41 33.

Restaurants: *** Luberon (with 16 rooms from 190 to 450 FF), 17 quai Léon-Sagy, Tel: (90) 74 12 50, complete meals from 130 to 360 FF.

Le Platane, Place Jules-Ferry, Tel: (90) 74 14 17, complete meals from.60 FF.

Brasserie Grégoire, 4 place Bouquerie, Tel: (90) 74 10 26, complete meals from 55 FF.

Shopping: Saturdays, there is an open market from 8 am to noon; wine: Cave Coopérative "Le Vin de Sylla" on N 100 at the west end of the city, Tel: (90) 74 05 39 (open Monday to Friday from 8:30 am to 12:30 pm and from 3 to 7 pm, Saturdays from 8 am); two large Supermarchées at the west end of town on N 100; Leclerc and Montlaur (both have inexpensive service stations), somewhat more toward the centre of town is a service station with lead-free fuel.

Sports Facilities: Riding Hotel Relais de Roquefure, Logis de France, Georges Rousset on N 100, Tel: (90) 74 22 80, offering accommodation and meals.
Transportation: There are a number of bus routes to Cavaillon, Avignon, Isle-sur-la-Sorgue, Manosque, Digne, Marseille, Aix-en-Provence, Bonnieux, Pertuis, Roussillon, Carpentras, Sault. More detailed information is available at the Tourist Information Office.
Important Addresses: Tourist Information Office, place Bouquerie/avenue Philippe de Girard, Tel: (90) 74 03 18.
Mairie: place Gabriel Péri, Tel: (90) 74 00 34.

Arles

Population: about 51,000; elevation: 9 metres (30 feet)
Arles lies about 37 km (23 miles) south of Avignon at the beginning of the Rhône Delta.

Arles / **History**

The first settlements in this area date back long before the Romans. Excavations in 1975 uncovered the remains of a Celtic-Ligurian settlement. The foundations of this city were first laid in the 6th century B.C. by the Greeks who came from Marseille and established a base in the swamp land. They named it "Arelate" meaning "the city in the swamps." The citizens of Arelate were very active in commerce and trade — even with the Romans, who would conquered the Provence beginning in 122 B.C. Arelate was of strategic importance not only because of its location on the Rhône, but because of its proximity to the sea as well. At that time it was even closer to the sea than today. The Romans quickly realised this potential and included Arelate into their network of roadways. The roads led over the Rhône bridge to Spain. The Roman commander Marius, who conquered the Teutons in 102 B.C., built a canal along the Rhône leading to the sea — he used this to secure the supplies for his troops. During a conflict between Pompeius and Caesar in 49 B.C., Arelate sided with Caesar and Marseille, with Pompeius. Because Caesar was victorious in this conflict, Arelate would enjoy a rapid development. This was especially true once Constantine chose Arelate as his residence in 314 A.D., ordered a council to Arelate and made it the bishop's seat as well as the capital of Gallia.

◀ *A view through the gateway arch in St-Saturnin d'Apt into the expanses of the Provençal landscape*

After the decline of the Roman Empire, the city fell under the turmoil of a number of tribes — the Visigoths and Ostrogoths, even the Normans — finally to be conquered by the Franconians under the leadership of Charlemagne. The city became the capital city of Charlemagne's extensive kingdom, also known as Arelate. This kingdom consisted of a portion of the Provence and formed the border to France after having been annexed by the Holy Roman Empire in 1032 A.D. The governing power lay in the hands of the bishops who represented the distant emperor. At the end of the 12th century, conflicts broke out in Arles and in many other towns in southern France. The call for the right to self-administration and association with the Italian city-republics could not be overheard. The archbishop fled after having relinquished his rights to the counts of Barcelona. The Spanish territory of the Provence vanquished the representatives of the emperor and ruled up to the marriage into the House of Anjou. The most famous of the counts of Anjou was King René; after his death, the heirs transferred ownership of the Provence to the French kingdom in 1481. Since that time, Arles was considered a provincial city. This was to change with the age of tourism — when Arles and art attracted the attention of the tourist industry. The 100 anniversary of the arrival of Vincent van Gogh in Arles was celebrated by the city in 1989 with numerous special events.

Arles / **Sights**

It is best to follow the signs to the centre of town "Centre Ville" and the "Office de Tourisme" and park on one of the tree-lined boulevards on the outer edge of the inner city. At the tourist office on the Boulevard des Lices, informational materials and city maps are available. For specific questions, the information office, located in the library will be of help. The Cité of Arles is easily explored on foot. Directly across from the Office de Tourisme, on can stroll through the Jardin Publique, a picturesque park with a monument to Vincent van Gogh — the only obvious reminder of this famous resident. Directly adjacent to the park is the Roman theatre. In the form of a semi-circle of ascending rows of seats, this theatre has a diameter of 103 metres (337 feet) and could hold up to 10,000 spectators. Farther along, one will see the amphitheatre Les Arènas. It was built in 46 B.C. and has an elliptical form. Performances still take place here today. Arles attracts visitors in summer with bullfights held in the Les Arènes, with animals from the bull-breeding region of Camargue *(→Bullfights)*. A little farther to the west is the Place de République. At the centre of the square, there is an Egyptian obelisk, which was found at the former Roman circus and was reerected by Louis XIV. Also on the Place de République is the Musée d'Art Païen (Museum for Pagan Art). It houses an important collection of Roman art and is housed in the former St-Annen Church from the 17th century. The impressive city hall (Hôtel de Ville) was built in the 17th century around a clock tower from the 16th century. Unpretentious in comparison is the former St-Trophime Cathedral. The cathedral was built on the foundations of a basilica from the 11th and 12th centuries in Romanesque style. A Gothic gallery was added in the 15th century. The cathedral was thoroughly renovated around 1870. The elaborate portal stands out from the simplicity of the exterior. Because of the narrow floor plan and the towering pillars, the interior appears colossal. Despite the valuable tapestries and marble sarcophagi, the sanctuary leaves an unembellished impression. To reach the cloister (cloître) one must go through the entrance next to the church. Unusually richly decorated with reliefs, this is the most famous and definitely most beautiful cloister in the Provence. Located on the Place du Forum are the ruins of the former forum which at one time extended all the way to the Place de République. On the Place du Forum, there is a monument in honour of Frédéric Mistral. Around the turn of the century, he invested the money from his Nobel Prize in the Museum of Local History (Muséon Arlatan). The museum has an extensive collection of regional articles such as clothing, handicrafts and furniture. It is housed in the former Palais Laval-Castellane, built in the 16th century. In the courtyard are the remnants of a Roman monument. This museum is very congenial, as the employees wear the beautiful costumes of the region. Somewhat further are the Constantine thermal baths, only parts of which have been preserved. During the time following the tourist season, it is worthwhile to visit the Musée Réattu, located opposite the Constantine baths. This museum is housed in a beautiful building from the 15th century. This command post of the Maltese Knights was later purchased by the painter Réattu (1760-1833), who later used it to display his own as well as other works by regional artists. The city of Arles later purchased the building. Today, there is a substantial collection of art, for example a donation from Picasso (57 drawings) who lived near Aix-en-Provence *(→ Vauvenargues).* Prominent photographic exhibitions are typical for this museum as well as the city of Arles: Arles is the seat of an international photographic society and has thus become a centre for photography. A historical sight is the graveyard Alyscamps. As early as during Roman times, there was a cemetery located here on one of the main axial streets of the city. Later in the 13th century, the cemetery became a coveted burial site for the Christians. The most impressive archaeological finds are now located in the Musée d'Art chrétian (Museum for Christian Art), housed in a former chapel from the 17th century near the Place de République. On the poplar-lined Allée des Sarcophages are only the less artistically sophisticated stone sarcophagi.

Arles / **Practical Information**

Accommodation

Hotels: **** Jules César (formerly an old monastery with cloister and inner courtyard; restaurant Lou Marquès), boulevard Lices, Tel: (90) 93 43 20, 55 rooms 350-800 FF.

*** D'Arlatan (without restaurant) rue Sauvage, Tel: (90) 93 56 66, especially attractive estate from the 15th century, decorated with beautiful furnishings, patio and garden, 42 rooms 298-598 FF.

** Forum (without restaurant), 10 place du Forum, Tel: (90) 93 48 95, 43 rooms.

* Le Cloître (without restaurant), 18 rue Cloître, Tel: (90) 96 29 50, 33 rooms 160-230 FF.

Camping: City, 67 route de Crau, Tel: (90) 93 08 86; 13 km (8 miles) west of Arles in Saliers, Camping-Caravaning Crin-Blanc, Tel: (66) 87 48 78; east of Arles in Pont-de-Crau Camping des Rosiers, Tel: (90) 96 02 12.

Automobile Repairs: BMW, Citroën, Mercedes and Toyota, Peugeot-Talbot, Renault, VW.

Entertainment: Evening folklore performances take place in the Antique Theatre, pilgrimage provençale, costume festivals, steer races; international nativity exhibits from December to January.

Medical Care: On-call medical care is available through the Gendarmerie, Tel: (90) 96 02 04; Hôpital van Gogh, Tel: (90) 93 98 55.

Restaurants: *** Lou Marquès (and Hotel Jules César), boulevard Lices, Tel: (90) 93 33 47; this restaurant is especially worth recommending due to its specialities, complete meals 185-345 FF.

** Vaccarès, place du Forum (first floor), Tel: (90) 96 06 17, complete meals 150-190 FF.

* Host. des Arènes, 62 rue Refuge, Tel: (90) 96 13 05, complete meals 60-90 FF.

Shopping: Wednesdays — grocery market; Saturdays general open market.

Transportation: Arles is easily accessible, located at the junction of N 113 and N 570. There are train connections to Lyon, Marseille, etc. Buses operate to Aix, Nîmes, Les Baux, Tarascon, Marseille and to the Camargue region.

Important Addresses

Tourist Information: boulevard des Lices, Tel: (90) 93 49 11 and in the Library, 35 Place de République, Tel: (90) 96 29 35.

Post Office: boulevard des Lices, Tel: (90) 96 07 80.

Artisanat

The term Artisanat is encountered in the Provence quite often. This means handicrafts in the broadest sense, for example a mason working with natural stone also falls under this heading.

Avignon

Population: about 93,000; elevation: 23 metres (75 feet)
Avignon lies approximately 37 kilometres (23 miles) north of Arles and 24 kilometres (15 miles) southwest of Carpentras. This city is the capital of the Département Vaucluse.

Avignon / **History**

The history of Avignon is closely tied to the Church, specifically with the popes. The city's history up to the 14th century was relatively uneventful. A power struggle between the Church and the French crown brought Avignon into the limelight. Although this period did not even last one hundred years (1309-1403), it was still important to the city of Avignon. At the beginning of the 13th century relations seemed to be harmonious between the Church and the French crown; Louis VIII and Pope Innocent III had combined forces against the separatist Albigensian sect. Employing a clever strategy, Louis VIII wanted to expand his empire to the Mediterranean, drawing the pope into a war of conquest. Owing to the fact that the Count of Toulouse had owned the Mediterranean land and because he not only tolerated but supported the sect, Louis VIII was able to recruit the pope for a holy war of sorts. After the king's victory in this conflict, the church was given Comtat Venaissin as a sign of gratitude. This period of peace between the Church and the French crown ended abruptly at the end of the 13th century. The cause of this were King Philip IV's (Philip the Fair's) plans to introduce the taxation of church property. The refusal and demand for worldly power by Pope Boniface VIII prompted Philip to arrest and imprison the pope. Pope Boniface VIII died shortly after being released from prison in 1305. His successor, the Archbishop of Bordeaux Clement IV, could not have been more favourable to the king if he had selected the new pope himself. This pope left Rome under the pretence that his safety could not be ensured there and returned to Avignon.

Avignon / **Sights**

Today, "the city of popes" is still almost entirely enclosed by a city wall measuring almost 5 kilometres (3 miles) in length and built from 1353 to 1370. In the

19th century, the former embattlement trenches were filled in. A boulevard was later built where these trenches once were and this is the best place to park. One can enter the city through seven gates or one of the additional passages through the wall which were added in the 19th century. The focal point of the city is the papal palace with a total area of 15,000 square metres (34,407 square feet) and was built from 1334 to 1352 during the time of the pontificates Pope Benedict XII and Pope Clement VI. This impressive Gothic building is similar to a fortress and is the destination of countless stalwart tourists today. The furnishings were plundered and destroyed during the French Revolution, the reason that most of the rooms stand empty. Through the use of the palace as barracks at the beginning of the 19th century, many of the frescoes were plastered over. Despite this, a few beautiful examples of the frescoes remain preserved and today, many of the high walls are covered with tapestries and Gobelins, which are not originally from the papal palace. Depending on the amount of time one has to spend here, one can take the fifty-minute tour or merely view a few of the rooms on one's own. Afterwards, one should take a stroll through the park laid out on a 60 metre (193 foot) high cliff behind the palace (Rocher des Doms). From the terraces, one can enjoy the beautiful view extending from the pretty suburb of Villeneuve-lès-Avignon up to Mont Ventoux and down the Rhône Valley with the famous bridge of Avignon, Pont Saint-Bénézet. Built by Jean Bénézet and the Brotherhood of Bridge Builders from 1177-1185, this bridge was once around 900 metres (2,943 feet) long with 22 arches. Today, it ends after the four remaining arches in the middle of the river. Also worth a visit is the Petit Palais near the papal palace, built in the 14th century, with a collection of Italian paintings. A stroll through the old city leads past magnificent façades, elegant entryways to the numerous Cardinals' Palaces and patrician houses from the 14th to 18th centuries. The Palais du Roure, located on Rue du Collège-du-Roure, has an entryway from the 15th century and houses an excellent library covering the culture and language of the Provence. Not far from here is the central square of the city, the Place de l'Horloge. Where the Roman forum once stood is not a group of impressive buildings: the city's theatre (1846-1847) and the city hall (1845) built around the old bell tower from the 14th to 15th century. A few steps from here is the Saint-Agricola Church. According to legend, this church was founded in the 7th century by Saint Agricola, the patron saint of Avignon, and was then reconstructed during the 14th century. The Saint-Didier Church (14th century) on Place Saint-Didier is the largest church in Avignon to have been built during the era of the popes. The massive building with its square tower is unembellished both inside as well as outside. This is an example of the Provençal Gothic architecture. Inside, there is a glass plate depicting the construction of the Saint-Bénézet Bridge. Among the city's museums, the Calvet Museum is especially worth recommending. Originally a private collection of paintings and library belonging to the benefactor Esprit Calvet (1729-1810), the museum, housed in a building from the 18th century, now has predominantly works from the 16th to 18th centuries as well as exhibitions on wrought iron. The Musée lapidaire exhibits finds from archaeological excavations dating back to the Roman and Gallo-Roman eras. For those interested in the history of printing, the Théodore-Aubanel-Musée exhibits fascinating printing tools and documents. The Aubanel Printing House, established during the 18th century, still exists today. In addition to an extensive collection of porcelain and ceramics, the Louis-Vouland Museum has a collection of French furnishings, predominantly from the 18th century.

Avignon / **Practical Information**

Accommodation

Hotels: **** D'Europe Vieille Fontaine, 12 place Crillon, Tel: (90) 82 66 92, an especially attractive residence from the 16th century, 43 rooms 390-900 FF, complete meals 155-200 FF.

*** Cité des Papes (without restaurant), 1 rue J.-Vilar, Tel: (90) 86 22 45, 63 rooms 290-360 FF.

** Bristol-Terminus (without restaurant), 44 cours Jean Jaurès, Tel: (90) 82 21 21, 91 rooms 162-360 FF.

* St-George (without restaurant), 12 rue de l'Etoile, Tel: (90) 88 54 34, 21 rooms 130-152 FF.

Camping: Bagatelle, Tel: (90) 86 30 39.

Pont-Saint-Bénézet, Tel: (90) 82 63 50.

In Le Pontet: Grand Bois-La Tapy, Tel: (90) 31 37 44.

Automobile Repairs: Alfa-Romeo, Austin-Rover, BMW, Citroën, Datsun-Nissan, Fiat, Lancia, Autobianchi, Ford, Mercedes-Benz, Peugeot-Talbot, Renault, VW.

Entertainment: Avignon is a centre for cultural events and conventions. Detailed information is available through the Office de Tourisme.

Medical Care: For on-call medical service, contact l'Hôtel de Police, Caserne de Salles, Tel: (90) 85 17 17.

S.O.S. Médecins, rue Campo-Bello, Tel: (90) 82 65 00.

Restaurants: *** Hiély (especially recommended because of its exquisite specialities, reservations are recommended), 5 rue République (mezzanine level), Tel: (90) 86 17 07, complete meals 160-260 FF.

** Le Vernet (with a lovely garden), 58 rue J.-Vernet, Tel: (90) 86 64 53, complete meals from about 150 FF.

* Salon de la Fourchette, 17 rue Racine, Tel: (90) 85 20 93, complete meals 100-140 FF.

Shopping: Daily, except Mondays, there is a weekly market Les Halles; flower market daily at place Pie and Saturday mornings at place des Carmes; flea market Sundays at place des Carmes.

Sports Facilities: Riding school La Barthelasse, chemin du Mont-Blanc, Le Barthelasse, Tel: (90) 85 83 48.

Transportation: Avignon is accessible by motorway (A7 and A9) and a number of train connections (For information on trains transporting cars, Tel: (90) 82 50 50). The airport is about 8 km (5 miles) southeast of the city, Tel: (90) 88 43 49, but only for domestic flights. A number of bus routes operate in the city.

Important Addresses

Tourist Information: 41, Cours Jean-Jaurès, Tel: (90) 82 65 11; Chambre départementale de tourisme de Vaucluse, La Balance, B.P. 20147, F-84008 Avignon Cedex.

Post Office: avenue Kennedy, Tel: (90) 82 99 40.

Banon

Population: 950; elevation: 770 metres (2,518 feet)

This town is worth visiting just for the view it offers of the Plateau de Vaucluse and Montagne de Lure. Banon is located approximately 32 kilometres (20 miles) north of Apt on the D 51, the approach into Banon in the Département Alpes-de-Haute-Provence. Banon is widely known for its goat cheese wrapped in chestnut leaves. The old city centre is partially abandoned.

Barbarotte

In the Provence, Barbarotte are the typical wrought iron enclosures on the church towers and city gates.

Barbegal

Three kilometres (2 miles) south of Fontvielle on the D 82 near Arles and Montmajour are the remains of an aqueduct and a flour mill driven by a water wheel, which supplied Arles with flour and water during the Roman period.

Barbentane

Population: approximately 3,000; elevation: 51 metres (167 feet)

The small town of Barbentane, located on the confluence of the Durance and Rhône rivers, makes a good place to spend the night for those who find the city of Avignon, located 10 kilometres (6¼ miles) to the north, too loud.

Barbentane / **Sights**

Barbentane is predominantly known for its castle from the 17th century. Located in an extensive park, it contains furnishings from the Louis-quinze (Louis V) and Louis-seize (Louis VI) period as well as various works of art. The city can be entered through one of the old city gates. Directly next to the 13th century church, which was expanded through a side aisle and a tower during the Middle Ages is the Maison des Chevaliers, the town hall from the 16th century with its famous gallery.

Barbentane / **Practical Information**

Accommodation: ** Castel Mouisson (without restaurant), quartier Castel-Mouisson, via route Rognonas approximately 1.5 km (1 mile), Tel: (90) 95 51 17, 16 rooms 210-230 FF.

* Négociants (without restaurant), cours Jean-Baptiste Rey, Tel: (90) 95 52 45, 10 rooms beginning at 130 FF.

* St-Jean, 1, cours Jean-Baptiste Rey, Tel: (90) 95 50 44, 14 rooms beginning at 115 FF, complete meals from 60 FF.

In addition, there is a large selections of Gîtes ruraux — information is available through the town hall.

Shopping: A market takes place every Wednesday.

Important Addresses: Tourist Information Office in the town hall (Mairie), Tel: (90) 95 50 39.

Bargaining

It is especially common (and fun) to bargain with prices right before the marketplaces close for the day. Also when shopping for antiques, the prices usually allow room for bargaining.

Beaches →*Camargue, Marseille*

Beaucaire

Population: approximately 13,000; elevation: 18 metres (59 feet)

Today, Beaucaire is a small centre for trade and commerce with a large industrial sector producing cement and wine as well as an electrical plant on the banks of the Rhône. The city is on the right banks of the Rhône, directly across from Tarascon and up until the 19th century, it was one of the most significant cities for trade fairs. Some of the buildings in the old city are evidence of this city's glorious past.

Beaucaire / **History**

The history of Beaucaire dates back to the Roman settlement of Ugernum and later fell under the rule of the Franconians, who further developed the city. During the Middle Ages, it was controlled by the Count of Toulouse. Through his establishment of a trade fair in the 13th century, the cornerstone was laid for Beaucaire's development into an important trade fair city. Visitors from near and far — some set the numbers at tens of thousands of people — travelled over the Rhône to Beaucaire. Owing to the fact that this city supported the Reformation, it experienced a fate similar to that of Les Baux. Richelieu had the Château and the fortifications razed. The city's reputation as a trade fair city was able to save the city from destruction well into the 19th century. After this, due to the construction of the railway, Beaucaire lost its significance.

Beaucaire / **Sights**

Across from the castle of Tarascon and separated from it by the Rhône River is the château, which was built in the 13th century. The two are surrounded by a park, dense with vegetation. During the persecution of the Protestants, Richelieu had it demolished in 1632. What remained were the Romanesque chapel, some ruins of the fortress and a tower. The former watch tower made from white stone (Beau Caïre) gave the city its name and is visible from quite a distance. In addition to two museums and several magnificent house façades, the Notre-Dame-des-Pommiers with its beautiful Baroque façade and the Hôtel de Ville (town hall) housed in a building from the 17th century are especially worth seeing. Nearby, approximately 4.5 kilometres (3 miles) toward Nîmes are the remnants of the Abbaye de St-Roman.

Beaucaire / **Practical Information**

Accommodation

Hotels: ** Les Doctrinaires, quai Gén.-de-Gaulle and 32 rue Nationale, Tel: (66) 59 41 32 (an old Collège from the 17th century), 34 rooms 280-330 FF, complete meals 95-195 FF.

* Vignes Blanches, route Nîmes southwest, Tel: (66) 59 13 12, 61 rooms 250-380 FF, complete meals 90-170 FF.

Camping: Le Rhodanien, Tel: (66) 59 25 50.

Automobile Repairs: Peugeot-Talbot.

Shopping: The market takes place on Thursdays and Saturdays.

Transportation: Train connections to Tarascon, Avignon.

Important Addresses

Tourist Information: 24 cours Gambetta, Tel: (66) 59 26 57.

Post Office: on rue Nationale.

Bédoin

Population: 1,840; elevation: 310 metres (1,014 feet)

Whether travelling via the D 974 from Carpentras or via the D 19 from Malaucène to reach the charming wine village on Mont Ventoux, there are ample panoramas to be enjoyed on either route. One attraction of the village is the church from the 17th century, furnished with Baroque altars. Also worth mentioning is the Romanesque Ste-Marie-Madeleine Church from the 11th century, somewhat further from the village on the D 19.

Bédoin / **Practical Information**

Accommodation

Hotel: Pins (modern accommodation), Tel: (90) 65 92 92, 25 rooms 220-250 FF, complete meals 70-90 FF.

Camping: Camping Municipal de la Pinède, Tel: (90) 65 61 03.

Nudist Camp Domaine de Bélézy, Tel: (90) 65 60 18.

Restaurants: ** L'Oustau d'Anaïs, route de Carpentras, Tel: (90) 65 67 43, complete meals 80-300 FF.

Sports Facilities: Gîte Equestre, Pierravon, Tel: (90) 65 61 10, room and board, swimming pool; La Bernarde, Tel: (90) 65 69 99, room and board Gîte rural; Riding School Le Ménèque, Tel: (90) 65 66 39.

Important Addresses: Office de Tourisme in the town hall (Mairie), Tel: (90) 65 60 08 and place Marché, Tel: (90) 65 63 95.

Bonnieux

Population: about 1,360; elevation: 335-425 metres (1,096-1,390 feet)
Approximately 47 kilometres (30 miles) east of Avignon and 13 kilometres (8 miles) southwest of Apt, this small, cozy mountain village is situated on the northern slopes of the Luberon mountain range.

Bonnieux / **Sights**

When walking through the steep alleyways up to the church, one should make a stop at the Bakery Museum. It has been fully refurbished and offers a historical account of everything which has to do with the main food staple so important to the Provence: bread. Beginning with a replica of a historical bakery as well as a collection of all former and present-day types of bread, a presentation of the development of the bread prices and even the wartime bread ration coupons. Located here is also the Office de Tourisme, with information on Bonnieux and the Provence in general. Continuing the climb up to the church from the 12th century (apsis and side aisles from the 15th century) there is a spectacular view of the Vaucluse Plateau. A stroll through the cedar forest is also worthwhile.

Bonnieux / **Practical Information**

Accommodation

Hotels: *** Hostellerie du Prieuré, rue J.-B. Aurard, Tel: (90) 75 80 78, an especially attractive, old priory from the 18th century with beautiful furnishings, 10 rooms 385-425 FF, complete meals 120-168 FF.
* César, place de la Liberté, Tel: (90) 75 80 18, 7 rooms 150-300 FF, complete meals 120-168 FF.
Six kilometres (three and three quarter miles) away on the D 36, D943 and a private road: *** L'Aiguebrun, Château de la Tour, Tel: (90) 74 04 14, located in a Luberon valley, 8 rooms 380-420 FF, complete meals 190 FF.
Chambres d'Hotes, Gîtes de France, Mme Mariette, 19 rue République, Tel: (90) 75 81 02, 5 rooms from 130 FF.
Camping: * Camping municipal du Vallon, route de Ménerbes, 150 sites, Tel: (90) 75 86 14.

Medical Care
Physicians: Dr. Fenelon, rue Voltaire, Tel: (90) 75 81 70, private number Tel: (90) 75 85 48; Dr. Souquet, Tel: (90) 75 81 70, private number Tel: (90) 75 90 99; Dentist M. Polluce, 4 rue Victor-Hugo, Tel: (90) 75 83 55.
Pharmacy: Pharmacie Lescure, rue Victor-Hugo, Tel: (90) 75 82 35; Ambulance Clerici, route de Marseille, Tel: (90) 75 80 45.
Restaurants: Le Fournil, 5 place Carnot, Tel: (90) 75 83 62.
Regain, 6 place du 4 Septembre, Tel: (90) 75 88 01.
Café Clerici (with rooms), place de 4 Septembre, Tel: (90) 75 82 20.
Salon de Thé, Henri Tomas, 9 rue de la République, Tel: (90) 75 85 52.
Shopping: Market on Fridays; Oudin, 1 rue de la Marie, sculptures, ceramics, jewellry, metals, pewter, wall hangings. Wine: Coopérative Vinicole de Bonnieux, Quartier de la Gare, Tel: (90) 75 80 03.
Bonnieux has a highly recommended wine coopérative (somewhat outside of town near the train station — the way is marked). Here, one can find the prize-winning, full-bodied Côtes du Ventoux A.O.C. and Côtes du Luberon V.D.Q.S, which are less expensive if purchased directly from the vat, "en vrac." Those who are not partial to the plastic canisters: the wine can also be purchased in practical aluminium containers, holding up to ten litres and of course, bottles as well.
Sports Facilities: Randonnées du Luberon, Bruno Rouan, Col Pointu, Tel: (90) 74 40 48, offering excursions on horseback.
Transportation: Taxi Marcel Pineau, Tel: (90) 75 85 98.
There are bus routes to Cavaillon, Apt and Aix/Marseille.
Important Addresses
Tourist Information: In the Bakery Museum Musée de la Boulangerie, rue République, Tel: (90) 75 88 34, or during the tourist season, at place Carnot, Tel: (90) 75 91 90.
Fire Department: Tel: (90) 75 80 60.
Gendarmerie/Police: Tel: (90) 75 80 77.
Mairie/town hall: Tel: (90) 75 80 06.
Post Office: Tel: (90) 75 80 00.

Bories

Bories are round constructions which are especially common near Gordes (Village noir). They often stand singly or in groups and are similar in shape to igloos. Built from stones and not using mortar, these constructions are known to many cultures and served as shelter as early as the Stone Age. Today, they are used mainly to stow equipment. Some bories originate from the 17th century; however, others have been constructed especially for the tourists. Some of the puzzles connected to these constructions and settlements remain unsolved even today since there are no cemeteries nor places of worship nearby.

Boulbon

Population: 830

Located along the D 91 between Avignon and Tarascon on an impressive rock formation is the village of Boulbon. The Château, built around 1400 by the count of the Provence, is surrounded by a massive fortress wall with several towers. After an easy climb to the castle which begins at the edge of the village, one can see the well preserved fortress with the remnants of its gardens. Somewhat outside the village is the cemetery with a beautiful chapel from the 12th century, which is impressive through its unpretentious architecture. Just as impressive is the Chapelle St-Julien, located about two kilometres (1¼ miles) from town. About 3 kilometres (2 miles) further is the →*St-Michel de Frigolet* Monastery, situated in a wooded valley.

Boule

Boule is a game that is very popular with the French. Thanks to the mild climate in the Provence, Boule can be played during almost the entire year. To play Boule, one needs only a large solid area free of stones on which metal balls can be thrown or rolled well. First, one small ball is positioned, which then serves as the target for the other balls tossed by the individual players. Each player attempts to toss his ball as close as possible to the target ball or to knock an opponent's ball farther away. Especially true for the Provence, this game is played exclusively by men. Each player has the right to judge the outcome. When the distances are not definitive, then they are carefully measured with a string. Often, there are organised tournaments which can become quite loud.

Bullfights

Regardless of one's views in regard to bullfights, this tradition remains an integral tradition of the south of France. There are two types of bullfights: the Portuguese fight, where the bull leaves the arena alive at the end of the bout and the Spanish Corrida, where the animal is killed. Both forms of bullfights are quite bloody and are therefore not for everyone.

Buoux

Population: 72; elevation 500 metres (1,635 feet)

Buoux, eight kilometres (5 miles) south of Apt and accessible via the D 113, is not easy to find. The town is almost completely abandoned today. Through a massive, rugged canyon, with alpine vegetation hanging on the canyon walls like tiny points of colour, one will pass a youth camp and cross a bridge before arriving at the parking area. From here, the ascent to Fort Buoux on the northern Luberon slopes begins. As early as the beginning of the Stone Age, the cliff of Buoux served in defence and later in the historical development, they were repeatedly used as a refuge for victims of persecution and a target for the occupiers. Ligurians, Albiquians and later the Romans made use of these natural fortifications. During the 14th and 15th centuries, the inhabitants of the village at the foot of the cliffs fled from the frequent enemy attacks onto the plateau. During the religious wars the Huguenot fort served in defence against the Catholic prosecution. By decree of Louis XIV in 1660, Richelieu levelled the fortress. Today, only the ruins of the fortifications, domiciles, storerooms dug directly into the rock and a well camouflaged stairway can be seen. The stairway leads directly into the valley basin. All of these constructions originated from different periods. About 2 kilometres (1¼ miles) from the fortress, one will find the famous Prieuré St-Symphorien Monastery which dates back to the 11th century. During the 12th century, this was renovated but today only the Romanesque bell tower has been preserved.

Restaurant: Auberge de la Loube, Quartier de la Loube (offering accommodation), Tel: (90) 74 19 58, complete meals from 120 FF.

Hotel: Auberge des Seguins, Auberge de France, Tel: (90) 74 16 37, 23 rooms 105-150 FF.

Business Hours

In the Provence, it can happen that one ends up standing before locked shop doors, even if one's travel guide, informational brochure or even the sign on the door says it should be open. It is simply not in accordance with the mentality in France, especially in the Provence, that one is dictated by regulations. For this reason, we do not include hours of operation for most of the museums etc.; this, because they are simply not definitive.

Because there is no legislation in France regulating business hours, most stores are open until 7 pm, some supermarkets are even open until 10 pm. On the other hand, hardly any stores are open continually. In rural areas, these times can vary. During the early afternoon (from noon to 2 pm) the entire country

takes a break and all stores, businesses and museums close for a few hours (for grocery stores, this may be ½ hour later).
Grocery stores are closed on Mondays, but are open on Sundays, usually until noon. *Supermarkets* are closed Sundays and are open Mondays. The weekend markets take place from 8 am to noon. *Wine Coopératives* are usually open Monday through Saturday from 8 am to noon and 2 to 8 pm. *Banks* do not have uniform business hours. Some are closed Mondays and open Saturdays and others vice versa. *Post Offices* are open Monday through Friday from 9 am to noon and 2 to 5 pm. *Tourist Information Offices* are usually open from 9 am to noon and from 2 or 3 pm to 6 pm. During the off-season they are often closed and only open if there is a demand. *Museums* are usually closed on Tuesdays, but not all of them. There is no admission 30 minutes before closing. Sometimes museums will open during the off-season if there is a demand. *Churches* are usually closed during lunchtime. *Hotels* and *Restaurants* have hours of operations depending on the season and have irregular hours during the winter months. Restaurants are usually closed one day during the week, this day differs from restaurant to restaurant.

An idyllic scene in the Provence: during midday the village seems almost deserted

Cadenet

Population: 2,640; elevation: 234 metres (765 feet)

Cadenet is some 23 kilometres (15 miles) south of Apt, taking the D943 at the foot of the Luberon.

One famous point of interest in the Gothic church is the baptistery which is said to have once been a Roman sarcophagus. The relief sculpture extending along the walls depicts a Bacchanal (a secret cult, with rituals in honour of Bacchus) which also supports the theory of the basin's origin. Scientists are not in agreement on this topic even today. The famous son of this city was André Etienne (1774-1838), who surrounded the outnumbering Austrian troops with a thunder of drumming during the battle in 1798, causing the Austrians to surrender, thinking that they were hopelessly outnumbered. Today the statue "Tambour d'Arcole" stands in his honour. Some ruins from medieval times and beautiful building façades round off the profile of this town. Other famous personalities from Cadenet include the composer Félicien David, born in 1810 and the Troubadour Elian de Cadenet, born in 1160.

Boule is more than merely a game, it also has its philosophical elements

Restaurant: ** Aux Ombrelles, Tel: (90) 68 02 40, with 11 rooms 90-195 FF, complete meals 75-190 FF.

Camargue

Originally, the region of Camargue was on the Rhône Delta. The landscape first changed with the arrival of the Romans. The forests were felled and the wood was used in the construction of ships. Over the course of the centuries, alluvial land built up due to the location between the Rhône and its tributary. Owing to these sedimentary deposits, the coastline continues to extend into the sea even today at a rate of 50 metres (164 feet) per year. In other areas such as Stes-Maries-de-la-Mer, in contrast, dikes had to be constructed to prevent the sea from claiming even more land. By draining the land and extracting salt, the attempt is being made to reclaim these regions. If this is successful, then this land will be used in the cultivation of rice or grapes. In the area near Aigues-Mortes are salt extraction pools which produce over 1.3 million tons of salt annually.

To routes can be recommended to drive to the Camargue region: from Arles via St-Gilles to Le-Grau-du-Roi, and the other, from Albaron to Stes-Maries-de-la-Mer. The following areas in the Camargue region are worth visiting:

Camargue / **Aigues-Mortes**

Aigues-Mortes is accessible from St-Gilles via the D 179/D 58. It is a town surrounded by swamp land and salt pools and has a population of around 4,500. Similar to St-Gilles, this town lives from one attraction.

History

The name of this town "Aquae Mortuae" stems from the Latin (dead water) and refers to the swamps. One can certainly imagine the reluctance of the soldiers and later the settlers when Louis IX chose the small town amid the swamps as a point of departure for the planned Crusades to Jerusalem. This was due to the lack of another, more appropriate Mediterranean port. First to be constructed was the canal to the Mediterranean, then a fortification wall with several towers and 10 gates was built around the town, which had meanwhile reached the dimensions of a city. The fortified city attracted not only pilgrims departing for the Holy Land. Up until the 14th century Aigues-Mortes had a population of almost 15,000. After the 6th Crusade in 1248, Louis IX set off for the 7th Crusade from Aigues-Mortes only to fall victim to the plague a short time later. In the years to follow, the canal to the Mediterranean was to see more and more traffic and with this, the significance of the city increased.

During the 17th century, the city sided with the Protestants and was drawn into the religious wars. With the development of the new Mediterranean harbour of Sète in the 18th century, the demise of Agues-Mortes seemed inevitable. The draining of the swamps, the subsequent cultivation of grapes (de Gris = sand-wine) and the extraction of salt ensured the livelihood of the city. Now, tourism supplements the city's income.

Sights

The city wall can already be seen from quite a distance, towering from the flat landscape. The wall encloses an area of over 1,600 square metres (17,223 square feet). A tour of the city can be best started at the Tour de Constance, which is located somewhat outside the city wall on the D 979 along the canal. It was constructed by Louis IX in 1248 before building the city wall and served as a watch tower. Its walls are six metres (20 feet) thick. After this it was used as a signal tower, and then as a prison during the following century. Many Protestants, after the Edict of Nantes was repealed, were imprisoned here for decades. The tower was connected by a bridge to the city wall during the 16th century. Points of interest include the knight's hall, where old documents are displayed. The view of the Camargue countryside from the observation platform in the tower is breathtaking (open daily from 9 am to noon and 2 to 6:30 pm in summer; 10 am to noon and 2 to 5 pm in winter). During a walk on the city wall, on will pass the ten gates and numerous towers. Here one can gain an overview of the city, laid out like a chess board. In addition, one will see the monument to Louis IX and the Notre-Dame-de-Sablons Church. Near this city on the D 179/D 46, is the Tour Carbonnière from the 14th century which served as an outpost. From the observation platform, there is a beautiful view of Aigues-Mortes. Three kilometres (2 miles) from Aigues-Mortes, heading toward Le-Grau-du-Roi are the salt pools Salins du Midi, which can be visited from July to August. More detailed information is available through the Office de Tourisme, Place Saint-Louis, Tel: (66) 53 73 00.

Camargue / **Le-Grau-du-Roi**

From Aigues-Mortes via the D 979, one will pass the Salins du Midi and reach the tourist city of Le-Grau-du-Roi with a population of about 4,000. Formerly a fishing village, today this city is stifled by the nearby holiday destination Le Grande Motte which attracts up to 100,000 tourists during the summer. La Grande Motte was built in the 1960's in futuristic architecture and offers extensive beaches, all types of aquatic sports, a casino, hotel complexes and a yacht harbour near Port-Camargue — everything that a tourist's heart could desire. For those looking for peace and quiet, this city cannot be recommended. Tourist Information: boulevard Front-de-Mer, Tel: (66) 51 67 70.

Camargue / **St-Gilles**

St-Gilles, the gateway to the Camargue region, is accessible via the N 572. The route leads through a pastoral landscape of fruit orchards and vineyards. With a population of almost 11,000, this town is now an agricultural centre and is widely known the façade and portals of its church.

History

The Greek saint Aegidius (Gilles in French) landed on the Camargue coast in the 8th century and lived as an ascetic in the swamp lands. There, he founded a Benedictine monastery and his grave became a destination for religious pilgrims. Owing to the city's location on a Rhône arm leading to the Mediterranean Sea, St-Gilles quickly became a popular point of departure for pilgrims setting off for the holy land. This lead to the increasing prosperity of the city. The build up of sand in this arm of the Rhône and the religious wars of the 16th and 17th century put an end to this development. The decline of this city was sealed by the French Revolution, during which the church was destroyed, leaving only the façade. It is exactly this façade which attracts the numerous tourists today.

Sights

As mentioned above, the main point of interest in St-Gilles is the church façade and portals. The church itself was built during the 12th and 13th centuries. What still stands does give an approximate impression of the massive dimensions that the entire church once had. The subdivision of the façade was influenced by Roman architecture, apparent form the arrangement of the columns. The five sculptures which embellish the main portal depict scenes from the life of Christ, while those around the three other portals are scenes from the Old and New Testament. Another point of interest is the bell tower which is all that remains of the chancels. The crypt, measuring 50 by 25 metres (164 x 82 feet) is spanned by one of the oldest Gothic arches in France. Inside the crypt, one can see various archaeological finds as well as a number of sarcophagi. Tourist Information: Maison Romane, Tel: (66) 87 33 75.

Camargue / **Stes-Maries-de-la-Mer**

The so-called capital of Camargue, Stes-Maries-de-la-Mer (population: 2,200) is accessible from Arles via the D 570. Stes-Maries was a city of rural character during the 1960's, which is now taken over by pilgriming gypsies in May. Observation of wild birds, horses and herds of steers is hardly possible anymore due to the constant growth of tourism over the last twenty years. This is especially true during the summer season when the city attracts 10,000 visitors.

History

As in many other villages of the Provence, the history of Stes-Maries' development is characterised by legends. According to the legends, several saints were stranded in this area in the year 40 A.D. Among these saints were the two Marys, Mary Jacobaea, the sister of the Mother of Jesus, and Mary Salome, the mother of the apostles John and Jacob, who were accompanied by their black servant Sarah. While the other saints separated and set off for other regions in the Provence, the two Marys and Sarah lived the rest of their lives here. Their bones were venerated as relics. Sarah became the patron saint of the European gypsies. The pilgrimage which takes place on the 24th and 25th of May has become a tourist attraction and the town is hopelessly overcrowded during this time.

Famous for its white horses: the Camargue

Sights

The church of pilgrimage, built in the 14th century and from the outside similar to a fortified castle, houses the sarcophagi of the two Marys in the upper chapel. The statue of Sarah stands in the crypt. It is carried to the sea during the pilgrimage processions. The church's fortifications can also be explored. A visit to the Baroncelli Museum with its folkloristic ambience is also very much worthwhile. From the roof terrace, there is a beautiful panorama of Camargue. Tourist Information: avenue Van Gogh, Tel: (90) 47 82 55.

Camargue / **Landscape and Wildlife**

Unfortunately, this region, located on the Rhône Delta in the marshy landscape, is no longer what it used to be 30 years ago. It has greatly suffered from the tourism. The conclusive and destructive marketing of the countryside which was once rich in wildlife, was countered at a relatively early stage through the nature reserve established around the Etang de Vaccarès. Only scientist with special permission are granted entrance to these areas in which numerous birds (for example, silver herons, flamingos, storks, bitterns in addition to countless ducks) can live undisturbed. In addition, there are the famous white horses and no less famous black steers which graze in the pastureland. For those interested in nature and wildlife, the local museum of Camargue on the D 570 between Arles and Avignon is recommended, offering photos, films and other documentation of the history of Camargue. The educational walking-tour, 3.5 kilometres (2 miles) in length, introduces the different areas of the Camargue region. Also worth mentioning is the ornithological park somewhat further on the D 570 when approaching Stes-Maries-de-la-Mer, in which numerous species of birds indigenous to the Camargue region can be seen.

Camargue / **Practical Information**

Accommodation: *Aigues-Mortes:* ** St-Louis, rue Admiral Courbet, Tel: (66) 53 72 68, 22 rooms 245-330 FF, complete meals 90-290 FF; * Croisades, modern accommodation without restaurant, 14 rooms 200-220 FF.

Le-Grau-du-Roi: * Acacias, 21 rue Égalité, Tel: (66) 51 40 86, 27 rooms 142-252 FF, complete meals 78-220 FF.

St-Gilles: * Cours, 10 av. F.-Griffeuille, Tel: (66) 87 31 93, 34 rooms 102-235 FF, complete meals 39-120 FF.

Stes-Maries-de-la-Mer: ** Lou Marquès (without restaurant), 6 rue Vibre, Tel: (90) 97 82 89, 14 rooms 179-215 FF; * Méditerranée (without restaurant), rue F.-Mistral, Tel: (90) 97 82 09, 14 rooms 120-210 FF.

Youth Hostel, located 9 km (5½ miles) from Stes-Maries-de-la-Mer: Hameau de Pioch Badet, Tel: (90) 97 91 72.
Automobile Repairs: Peugeot (Aigues-Mortes, St-Gilles), Renault (Aigues-Mortes).
Beaches: The portions of the beach near Stes-Maries-de-la-Mer in the vicinity of town are unfortunately overcrowded during tourist season.
Restaurants: *Aigues-Mortes:* ** Arcades (with 7 rooms from 450 to 500 FF), 23 boulevard Gambetta, Tel: (66) 53 81 13, complete meals 95-160 FF.
Le-Grau-du-Roi: * Le Palangre, 56 quai Ch.-de-Gaulle, Tel: (66) 51 76 30, complete meals 75-192 FF.
St-Gilles: * La Rascasse, 16 av. F.-Griffeuille, Tel: (66) 87 42 96, complete meals 58-90 FF.
Stes-Maries-de-la-Mer: *** Brûleur de Loupes, av. G.-Leroy, Tel: (90) 97 83 31, complete meals 150-180 FF; * Impérial, pl. Impériaux, Tel: (90) 97 81 84, complete meals 92-130 FF.
Sports Facilities: Tours accompanied by guides are offered along the marshlands. There is good fishing along the coast and in the Rhône, steam ship and boat excursions are offered on the sea and along the Petit Rhône as well as tennis courts, miniature golf etc.
Important Addresses: Office de Tourisme: Aigues-Mortes, place St-Louis, Tel: (66) 53 73 00; Le-Grau-du-Roi, boulevard Front-de-Mer, Tel: (66) 51 67 70; St-Gilles, Maison Romane, Tel: (66) 87 33 75; Stes-Maries-de-la-Mer, avenue Van Gogh, Tel: (90) 47 82 55.

Camping

The Provence is a camper's paradise. Everywhere there are signs directing one to camping areas. Camping areas are categorised — like the hotels in France — by one to four stars. Another option is to camp on farms (Camping Rural). One drawback is that the camping areas are hopelessly overcrowded during the summer months making advance reservations imperative. Camping just anywhere is strictly forbidden in the Provence. During the hot and dry summer months, fires can spread rapidly and are the cause of devastating damage each year. For this reason, open fires are strictly forbidden. Penalties for open fires are severe fines. A careless flick of the cigarette in a dry field can start a massive fire.
Information on camping and camping areas can be obtained through the local tourist information offices or from:

Fédération française de Camping-Caravaning, 78 Rue de Rivoli, F-75000 Paris, Fédération méditerranée de l'Hôtellerie de Plein Air, 2 rue Beauvau, F-13003 Marseille.

Car Rental

The national and international car rental agencies like Avis, Europcar, interRent and Hertz can be found in all of the larger cities usually located near the train stations or airports. Here it is possible to rent a car by the day or by the week without any problem. There are also budget rates on weekends for example. It is also possible to reserve a vehicle in advance from one's home country. The rental is invoiced using a basic rate plus kilometre charges. In addition, 33.33% tax is charged on the total. Insurance is usually not included in the price.

Carpentras

Population: 25,000; elevation: 100 metres (327 feet)
Carpentras is situated 24 kilometres (15 miles) north of Avignon, approximately 36 kilometres (22½ miles) south of Mont Ventoux. The former capital city of Comtat Venaissin was already an important hub for traffic in the Provence during the Roman times as well as being a centre for the cultivation of fruits and vegetables. This bishop's city was a Holy See up until the 18th century. After the French Revolution, Carpentras lost most of its significance. Today, Carpentras is once more an agricultural centre in France.

Carpentras / **History**

As the capital city of a Celtic tribe, the Cavarians, the city was expanded by the Romans under Augustus. Carpentras changed ownership quite often during the course of the centuries, until finally falling under the rule of the Avignon popes in 1274 and becoming the capital of Comtat Venaissin. The popes selected the city of Carpentras as their favoured residence, which consequently accelerated its growth so that in the 14th century, its city wall built in the early Middle Ages was expanded by a second, significantly larger one. With the return of the popes to Rome, and later through the French Revolution, Carpentras lost importance.

Carpentras / **Sights**

Quite pleasantly, Carpentras is not a centre for tourism, making it possible to discover the normal lifestyle. The Cathedral St-Siffrein from the 15th century houses some works by the sculptor Bernus of Mazan (1650-1728). Also worth seeing is the Palace of Justice from the 17th century (tours are possible on weekdays) and the nearby Roman Arch of Triumph (20 A.D.) with a beautiful eastern façade. Housed in the Hôtel d'Allemand, a palais from the 18th century, is the extensive and fascinating Bishop Malachie d'Inguimbert's library (230,000 volumes of which 80,000 are antique and 4,000 manuscripts and incunabula). There is a beautiful view of Mont Ventoux from the terrace on Place du 8 Mai on the northern city ring. In the Hôtel Dieu, one of the hospitals founded by Bishop d'Inguimbert in the 18th century, is especially worth seeing because of its pharmacy with beautifully painted cabinets and Moustiers-Fayencen. Also worth a visit is the oldest synagogue in France, built in the 15th century, rebuilt in the 18th century and fully restored today. The two-story building houses a bakery, in which the unleavened bread was baked, and the pools for ritual baths.

Carpentras / **Practical Information**

Accommodation: ** Fiacre (without restaurant), 153 rue Vigne, Tel: (90) 63 03 15, 20 rooms 160-300 FF.

* Le Coq Hardi, 36 place de la Marotte, Tel: (90) 63 00 35, modern accommodation, 19 rooms 145-260 FF, complete meals 78-160 FF.

Automobile Repairs: Citroën, Fiat, Ford, Peugeot-Talbot, Renault, VW.

Restaurants: ** La Rapière du Comtat, 47 boulevard du Nord (across from Porte d'Orange), Tel: (90) 67 20 03, complete meals 55-130 FF.

* Vert Galant, 12 rue Clapiès, Tel: (90) 67 15 50, complete meals 70-100 FF.

Shopping: The market takes place on Fridays; wine: Caveau des Vins, Place de Théâtre, Union des Vignerons des Côtes du Ventoux, 256, boulevard Naquet.

Sports Facilities: Riding School Centre équestre de Saint Ponchon, Tel: (90) 60 08 40.

Important Addresses: Office de Tourisme, 170 avenue Jean-Jaurès, Tel: (90) 63 00 78 and (90) 63 57 88.

Castellet

The small town of Castellet, southeast of Apt about 7.5 kilometres (5 miles) beyond Saignon on the D 48 offers: excursions on horseback and Gîte equestre, Camp de Bardons, Madeleine Namgeot, on the D 48, Tel: (90) 75 20 87; Camping (200 sites), room and board, swimming pool.

Cavaillon

Population: 21,000; elevation: 75 metres (245 feet)
Cavaillon is located 24 kilometres (15 miles) east of Avignon on the Durance.

Cavaillon / **History**

Today this city is a popular destination for excursions because of the beautiful views. The St-Jacques Hill was once the location of the first Ligurian settlement. During the fourth century B.C., the Cavarians raised the status to Oppidum, their holy city and engaged in trade and commerce with the Greek settlement of Massalia (Marseille). During their conquests, the Romans destroyed Oppidum and founded their city of Cabellio on the plain at the base of the hill. During its history, this city endured a difficult fate. Attacks by the Goths and the Arabs, the Albingensian wars and the plague had a devastating effect on the city. Cavaillon also being a part of the Comtat Venaissin, the city fell under the ownership of the popes, as similar to Carpentras. Today, Cavaillon enjoys the reputation of being the most important hub for agricultural products in the entire region.

Cavaillon / **Sights**

The relatively small cloister of the former Saint-Véran Cathedral, originally built in the 12th century and repeatedly rebuilt is — in addition to the cloister of St-Trophime in Arles — possibly the most beautiful of its kind in the Provence because of its intimacy. After being heavily damaged, it was renovated in the 17th century (open only during the morning). The synagogue on Rue Raspail offers insight into the significance of the Jewish community over this city's history. In the Rococo building from the 18th century, there is a small Jewish museum with various cultural exhibits. One example is the old oven used in baking the unleavened bread. Also interesting is a visit to the Archaeological Museum (Musée archéologique) which is housed in a Rococo chapel from the 18th century. This museum has a collection of prehistoric and Gallo-Roman finds. The only construction dating back to the Antique period are the ruins of a Roman triumphal arch dating back to the reign of Caesar Augustus. Not far from here, on St-Jacques Hill is the St-Jacques Chapel. From this vantage point on Mont Caveau, there is a magnificent panorama.

Cavaillon / **Practical Information**

Accommodation

Hotels: *** Christel, 2 km (1¼ miles) south of town, Tel: (90) 71 07 79, modern accommodation, 105 rooms 310-400 FF, complete meals 120-170 FF.

** Parc (without restaurant), place du Clos, Tel: (90) 71 57 78, 40 rooms 130-220 FF.
* Arilys, modern accommodation, 175 avenue Pont, Tel: (90) 76 11 11, 35 rooms 220-255 FF, complete meals 70-110 FF.
Camping: Camping de la Durance, Tel: (90) 71 11 78.
Automobile Repairs: Citroën, Ford, Peugeot-Talbot, Renault.
Entertainment: Cavaillon offers numerous cultural activities. In addition to many festivals pertaining mainly to the local folklore, the Centre Culturel et de Loisirs on rue du Languedoc, Tel: (90) 78 30 73, offers a diverse programme, including theatre performances, concerts from classical to jazz and ballet.
Restaurants: *** Prévot, 353 avenue Verdun, Tel: (90) 71 32 43, complete meals 139-285 FF.
** Nicolet (excellent specialities), 13 place Gambetta (second floor), Tel: (90) 78 01 56, complete meals 130-180 FF.
Five kilometres (3 miles) outside of town on the D2 in Robion: ** Maison de Samantha, Tel: (90) 76 55 56, complete meals 80-160 FF.
Shopping: The market takes place on Mondays and Fridays.
Sports Facilities: Two swimming pools; tennis courts.
Transportation
Train connections to Marseille, Avignon, Lyon, Pertuis.
Bus routes to Aix, Avignon, Beaucaire, Bonnieux, Carpentras, Gordes, Marseille, Pertuis, Saint-Rémy, Salon, Tarascon (bus terminal, Tel: (90) 78 32 39).
Important Addresses: Office de Tourisme, 79 rue Saunerie, Tel: (90) 71 32 01.

Céreste

Population: 850; elevation: 385 metres (1,259 feet)
Céreste is 18 kilometres (11¼ miles) from Apt on the N 100 in the Département of Alpes-de-Haute-Provence. It is a small town of Roman origin (Catuiaca) which has not yet been discovered by many tourists. With the exception of the ruins of the old fortification wall, Céreste offers the opportunity to observe the lifestyle of a Proveçale village. Céreste is also considered a good destination for fossil hunters, who might stumble on significant finds in the surrounding regions.

Céreste / **Practical Information**

Accommodation: ** L'Aiguebelle, Place de la République, Tel: (92) 79 00 91, 13 rooms 130-190 FF, complete meals 50-135 FF.
Automobile Repair: Renault, Tel: (92) 79 01 87.

Medical Care

Physician: Dr. André, boulevard J.-Jaurès, Tel: (92) 79 00 25.

Dentist: Michel Gontard, place de la République Tel: (92) 79 00 46.

Pharmacy: boulevard J.-Jaurès, Tel: (92) 79 02 80.

Restaurants: Restaurant de la Fontaine, pizzeria, cours Aristide-Briand, Tel: (92) 79 00 10.

Sports Facilities: Tennis courts.

Important Addresses

Office de Tourisme: Mme Mercey, Tel: (92) 79 03 99.

Taxi: cours Aristide-Briand, Tel: (92) 79 00 21.

Fire Department: Tel: (92) 79 00 21.

Gendarmerie/Police: Tel: (92) 79 00 01.

Châteauneuf-du-Pape

Population: 2,100; elevation: 117 metres (383 feet)

Châteauneuf-du-Pape is located 18 kilometres (11¼ miles) north of Avignon halfway to Orange. This town is famous for the wine it produces. The history of the famous vineyards goes back to the 14th century when Avignon became the seat of the popes. Châteauneuf-du-Pape was the summer residence of the popes. The cultivation of wine was instated by Pope John XXII and the wine produced was very popular in the papal courts. Pope John XXII also had the fortress built. Only a tower and some remnants of the wall remain of the fort. The Wine Museum, Caves du Père Anselme (admission free of charge, Tel: (90) 83 07 70), exhibits equipment and other tools used in the production of wine.

Châteauneuf-du-Pape / **Practical Information**

Accommodation

Hotel: ** Le Logis d'Arnavel (modern accommodation), 3 km (2 miles) via the D17, Route de Roquemaure, Tel: (90) 83 73 22, 15 rooms 230-260 FF.

Hotel-Restaurant La Garbure, 3 rue Joseph-Ducos, Tel: (90) 83 75 08, 5 rooms 190 220 FF.

Hôtel Mère Germaine, Tel: (90) 83 70 72, 6 rooms 100-130 FF.

Camping: Islon Saint-Luc, Tel: (90) 83 76 77.

Entertainment: This region attracts a good number of tourists and offers diverse entertainment. In addition to its traditional wine festivals (St. Mark Festival and introduction of the new vintage), the votive festival (first Sunday in July) and the musical evenings in July and August, there are many other festivals, exhibits etc.

Medical Care

Physicians: 27, rue Anselme-Mathieu, Tel: (90) 83 70 92.

Pharmacy: avenue Cdt-Lemaitre, Tel: (90) 83 71 61.

Restaurants: *** Host. Château des Fines Roches (Estevenin), 3 km (2 miles) via the D 17 on a private road, especially good specialities, situated in the wine region, reservations are recommended, with 17 rooms 520-720 FF, Tel: (90) 83 70 23, complete meals 195 FF.

Le Pistou, rue Joseph Ducos, Tel: (90) 83 71 75, complete meals from 80 FF.

Shopping: The market takes place on Fridays; wine: Jean Versino, Tel: (90) 83 73 60.

Sports Facilities: Hiking in the surrounding regions, swimming (pools open from June to September), tennis, fishing and excursions on horseback.

Important Addresses

Office de Tourisme: place du Portail, Tel: (90) 83 71 08 (closed Sunday and Monday mornings and in November).

Town Hall: rue Joseph-Ducos, Tel: (90) 83 70 92.

Cheval Blanc

The small, unpretentious town of Cheval Blanc lies 4.5 kilometres (3 miles) southeast of Cavaillon on the D 973 and has a church from the 17th century. Accommodation: Horseback Riding Hotel, excursions on horseback, camping, tennis, swimming pool, Camping des Genêts, Chemin de la Grande Bastide, Tel: (90) 78 36 87.

Children

Children are especially welcome in the Provence. The reputation that the southern Mediterranean countries have in regard to children also applies to the Provence. Discounts in museums, children's portions in restaurants etc. are commonplace.

Climate

In the Provence, the very hot summer months with temperatures exceeding 30 °C (87 °F) are quite tolerable because of the low humidity. During the mild winter months, in which frost and snow are only occasional occurrences, temperatures can climb to 20 °C (68 °F). In spring and autumn, sudden rain showers can flood the streets. During any season, the notorious cold mistral winds can sweep over the countryside following a number of days with calm winds. Originating in the northern mountains, these winds blow over the Provence toward the sea lowering temperatures up to 10 °C (50 °F). Despite sunny weather, the air temperatures can be icy and this can last for several days. One should, therefore, pack appropriate →*Clothing.* Preferred seasons for travel to the Provence are, of course, spring, summer and autumn. During the spring (March to May) the Provence is in full bloom with temperatures that are already pleasant. The height of summer (June to August) is not for everyone with very high temperatures. In addition, one should consider that the French also have holidays during July and August and enjoy travelling in their own country. This makes for hopelessly overcrowded motorways, hotels and campsites. Autumn (September to October/November) can be recommended, when temperatures have once again dropped into the comfortable range.

Clothing

The variable climate of the Provence makes it necessary to pack appropriate clothing. When the chilly mistral winds cause the temperatures to drop, warm clothing is essential (a sweater, wind-breaker, wool jacket and/or scarf). In addition, it is a good idea to bring sturdy shoes, especially when hiking in Les Baux. One should not underestimate the intensity of the sun even with the cool mistral winds. One must be careful in order to avoid a sunburn. A sun hat is practical for the Provence and long trousers and long-sleeve shirts and blouses will protect against biting insects.

Consulates →*Embassies*

Coustellet

The unpretentious town of Coustellet is 9 kilometres (5½ miles) north of Cavaillon at the junction of the N 100 and the D 2. The colourful marketplace on Sundays is worth recommending.

Coustellet / **Practical Information**

Accommodation: Hôtel Le Sarrat, Tel: (90) 76 85 58, 5 rooms 100-120 FF.
Restaurants: * Lou Revenent (with 15 rooms 160-250 FF), Tel: (90) 76 91 21, complete meals 75-135 FF.
Shopping: A fresh produce market takes place every Sunday from 8 am to noon. In comparison to the other open markets in Apt, Gordes or Isle-sur-la-Sorgue, this market is the most authentic. At this market, the farmers sell

agricultural produce and not any souvenirs. Wine: Cave Coopérative Maubec-Gare, Cave Coopérative Maubec-Luberon.

Crime

An unfortunate topic is the crime rate of the Provence which is on the rise. The constantly increasing rate of unemployment is most likely the main reason for this development. Where tourism is prevalent, thieves are never far away. The increasing stream of tourists to the Provence is, therefore, an ideal environment for thieves. For this reason, one should be cautious rather than overly trusting. At many of the parking areas there are signs in a number of languages warning against theft. One should not prominently display valuables. Always securely lock vehicles and look around to see if anyone is showing an inappropriate level of interest in the vehicle.

Cucuron

Population: 1,400; elevation: 375 metres (1,226 feet)
Cucuron is located around 8 kilometres (5 miles) east of Lourmarin on the D 27. This is a quaint little town with a number of fountains. According to legend, Caesar asked "Cur currunt" (why are you fleeing) when the residents fled as he approached the town — one original explanation of the town's name.

Cucuron / **Sights**

Cucuron has a long history. This is evident through the many finds dating back to Roman times. Some of these are on display in the small local museum housed in the former Hôtel de Bouliers from the 17th century (temporarily closed for renovations). Further up is the Notre-Dame de Beaulieu. The town also has remnants from a fortification wall dating back to the 12th and 16th centuries. The massive entry gate from the 16th century is now a clock tower. Above the town is a small castle with a tower dating back to the 14th century. This vantage point offers a beautiful view all the way to the Saint-Victoire massif on the horizon.

Cucuron / **Practical Information**

Accommodation: * L'Etang (modern accommodation), Tel: (90) 77 21 25, 8 rooms 180 FF, complete meals 110-200 FF.
Sports Facilities: Riding Hotel Gîte pédestre, équestre "La Rasparine," Régis and Micheline Bremond, Tel: (90) 77 27 68, room and board offered.

Cuisine

For many visitors to France, the food is the most important topic. The Provence offers culinary delights using the ingredients produced locally. Rich in aromatic herbs *(→Herbs and Spices),* fine vegetables and fruits and exquisite seafood (fruit de mer), the Provence has an abundance of specialities to tempt the palate. It is also said that the mutton from the Provence already has a flavour typical of the Proveçale herbs since the sheep graze on these herbs. Those who enjoy garlic will feel right at home in the Provence: the cuisine of the Provence makes use of a large proportion of garlic and is famous for Aïoli — a type of garlic mayonnaise. Gourmets will delight in a speciality that is relatively rare: truffles. These mushrooms grow below the earth on the roots of oak trees. Finding truffles has long since advanced to an art form, using specially trained dogs or pigs. Once found, the location of the truffles is a well-kept secret. Yet another important aspect of the regional cuisine is the *→wine.* Surrounded by vineyards, it would simply be a pity to chose an imported wine from the wine list. The ample sunshine in the Provence guarantees the highest en-

A panorama above the small village of Cucuron, the southern gateway to the Luberon mountain range

joyment, and where else does the wine taste so good as in the region in which it is produced?
A tasty tip for those travelling in the Provence is the locally produced honey.
Some important terms and phrases:

breakfast	petit déjeuner
lunch	déjeuner
supper	dîner
coffee with milk	café au lait
- with cream	- au crème
tea	thé
The bill, please.	L'addition, s'il vous plaît.

Customs Regulations

Visitors are allowed to take up to £270 ($475) worth of goods out of France within the EC. Included in this sum are goods bought and used in France,

The excellent wines are the result of the sunny climate of the Provence

for example articles of clothing. Within the EC, persons over 17 years of age may bring the following into France: 300 cigarettes or 150 cigarillos or 75 cigars or 400 g of tobacco and 1.5 l of spirits over 22%, 3 l under 22%, 3 l of dessert wine or sparkling wine, 5 l of other wines. The receipts should be saved as proof of the price paid for the wine; a agricultural compensation tax of 3 to 7 p (6 to 12 cents) per bottle is levied. Duty-free for persons over 15 years of age are: 1 kg of coffee or 400 g of coffee extract as well as 200 g of tea and 60 g of tea extract. Perfume up to 75 g and Eau de Toilette up to .375 l is also duty-free.
Those who meet these requirements can merely go by the customs area with the green "E." One should, however, be prepared for occasional spot checks by the customs officers.

Départements

The Provence is composed of the following Départements or parts thereof. These numbers are also on the licence plates of automobiles and are the first two numbers of the five-digit postal codes as well.
04 Alpes-de-Haute-Provence; 06 Alpes-Maritimes; 13 Bouches-du-Rhône; 30 Gard; 83 Var; 84 Vaucluse.

Discounts

Many of the museums offer special group rates and discounted admission for children. When presenting the appropriate identification, artists, journalists and teachers are also eligible for a discount. In addition, some cities (Arles, for example) offer inexpensive combined admission tickets for all of the museums. One can also count on discounted hotel prices during the low season and if staying for more than one night.

Donjon

Donjon, meaning lord's tower, is the term for the main tower of the medieval castles.

Economy

As in many Mediterranean countries, the main branch of the economy in the southern regions of France is agriculture. The production of wine and cultivation of vegetables in the Provence was already started by the Greeks and Romans. During the Middle Ages, when King René (1408-1480) imported the muscatelle grape and the mulberry bush (important for breeding silkworms), the Provence experienced an economic boom. This became apparent through the establishment of a trade fair in Beaucaire during the Middle Ages. The Rhône basin with its good climate, rich soil and abundant water, rapidly became a centre for the production of fruit and vegetables, making it the most important area for these products in France. The products are transported to the rest of France and other countries in the European Community. The important region for grain and livestock is the Crau Plain surrounding Arles. The production of wine, with its famous rosés, is an important economic factor in the Provence. The Provence has relatively few natural resources with the exception of ochre, bauxite and limestone deposits. These were neglected in regard to industrial development by the central government in Paris well into the 20th century. Today, especially around Marseille and the crude oil port of Fos, there are operative petro-chemical, iron and steel producing industries. The harbour of Marseille has developed into the second largest in Europe after Rotterdam. In other areas in the Provence, light industry developed like food processing, fruit processing and cement factories. Today, the water power of the Rhône and Durance Rivers are tapped by hydro-electric power plants. The two power plants Marcoule and Pierrelatte on the Rhône ensure a consistent energy supply. Significant in the economic development over recent years has been the strong increase in tourism, which in Camargue, for example, also has its negative aspects.

Electricity

The voltage in France is 220 V. If one requires an adapter (adapteur), these can be purchased in France without any problems. Strangely enough, the sockets even within one room are not always the same.

Also, despite the most modern technology and overproduction of electricity by French atomic reactors, there are still frequent power outages in the Provence. One will notice the butane and propane canisters available at almost every service station. Since electricity is relatively expensive, the most important household appliances run on gas.

Embassies

If problems arise or travel documents lost, then it is best to contact the embassies in Paris.

Great Britain: 35, rue du Faubourg-St-Honoré, 8ème, Tel: 42 66 91 42.

United States: 2, av. Gabriel, 8ème, Tel: 42 96 12 02. For lost passports contact the Office of American Services, 2, rue St-Florentin, Tel: 42 96 12 02, ext. 2613, located three blocks from the embassy.

Canada: 35, av. Montaigne, 8ème, Tel: 47 23 01 01.
Australia: 4, rue Jean Rey, 15ème, Tel: 45 75 62 00.
New Zealand: 7ter, rue Leonard-de-Vinci, 16ème, Tel: 45 00 24 11.

Emergency

In case of emergency, contact the police or the local Gendarmerie, which both have information on local doctors, pharmacies and hospitals. Otherwise the embassies in Paris can also help further. If one has problems on the motorways or is involved in an accident, the police can be reached using the telephones located along the motorways, or by dialling the emergency number 17.
Police-secours (emergency number): Tel: 17
Fire Department (Pompiers): Tel: 18
On-call physician in Arles: Tel: (90) 96 11 21
On-call physician in Avignon: Tel: (90) 85 17 17
On-call physician in Marseille: Tel: (91) 52 84 85
Centre anti-poison (poison centre) in Marseille: Tel: (91) 75 25 25.
→*Embassies, Police, Medical Care*

Entertainment

Those who want to go where things are happening and a lot of activities are offered should choose the Côte d'Azur over the Provence. The Côte d'Azur offers a broad selection of every type of entertainment. The entertainment scene in the Provence is subdued in comparison. In the Provence, there are no night clubs and it is better that way. Naturally, the people of the Provence enjoy entertainment as well, but this usually takes on the form of folklore events. Throughout the entire Provence, there is an abundance of holidays and festivals, whether religious holidays, wine festivals, summer festivals, harvest festivals etc. Every opportunity to celebrate is taken advantage of. Old traditions are upheld, for example folk dancing in costumes typical to the Provence. Much is also offered in the area of music and theatre. The Provence has become a very attractive region for its concerts, festivals and theatre performances. The tourist information offices offer a wealth of informational material on the numerous special events.
→*Holidays and Celebrations*

Equipment

No special equipment is necessary for a trip to the Provence. However, a pocket lamp often comes in handy when visiting grottoes or crypts. Binoculars will also be an asset when considering the beautiful scenery and panoramas from observation points.
→*Clothing*

Eygalières

Eygalières lies 12 kilometres (7½ miles) east of St-Rémy halfway to Cavaillon via the D 99 and D 74.
It was named Aquileria by the Romans because of its springs (aqua = water), and it is an excellent example of a terraced village typical of the Provence. Somewhat outside of the village is the St-Sixte Chapel. The apsis originates from the 12th century, and from here there is a beautiful view of the Alpilles.

Eygalières / **Practical Information**

Accommodation
Hotels: *** Mas de la Brune, 1.5 km (1 mile) via the D 74A, Tel: (90) 95 90 77, (very attractive estate from the 16th century with an adjacent park), 10 rooms 575-695 FF, complete meals 260-345 FF.
** Crin Blanc, 3 km on the D 24B, Tel: (90) 95 93 17, modern accommodation, 10 rooms 280 FF, complete meals 150-220 FF.
Camping: Les Oliviers, Tel: (90) 95 91 86.
Automobile Repairs: Citroën Garage Barrouyer, Tel: (90) 95 90 83.
Restaurants: ** Auberge Provençale (with 4 rooms 190-310 FF), Tel: (90) 95 91 00, complete meals 160-180 FF.

Eyguières

Eyguières is a town at the base of the Alpilles near Salon-de-Provence. It is accessible via the D 569 and has an atmosphere typical for the Provence with numerous fountains and the ruins of a fortification wall. The town is surrounded by olive groves.

Famous People of the Provence

The famous Dutch painter Vincent van Gogh (1853-1890) lived for one year and painted in Arles. Here, he was visited by his colleague Paul Gauguin (1848-1903). In 1889, van Gogh went into the asylum of St-Rémy-de-Provence for about one year. The great painter Paul Cézanne (1839-1906) did live for a long time in Paris, but returned to Aix-en-Provence where he was born and spent the years of his youth. Probably the most famous painter of our time, Pablo Picasso (1881-1973), lived the last years of his life in his castle in Vauvenargues, where his grave is located today. In Gordes and Aix-e-Provence are Museums for the Hungarian painter Victor Vasarely (born in 1908), who made the Provence to his home. Near Gordes, the versatile artist Frédérique Duran, famous for her stained glass windows, among other works has established a museum for glass art. Many of her works can be seen here. The Italian author Francesco Petrarca (1304-1374), who lived part of his life in Arles, returned to Fontaine-de-Vaucluse for 16 years. The first thing he did was to climb Mount Ventoux. Alphonse Daudet (1840-1897), the author of "Tartarin of Tarascon," was born in Nîmes and often lived in Fontvielle, where the "Daudet Mill" is found today. In order to preserve the language and culture of the Provence, Frédéric Mistral (1830-1914, born in Maillane) used the money from his Nobel Prize to finance the establishment of a museum dedicated to local culture in Arles. Marcel Pagnol (1895-1974) an author born in Aubagne (Marseille) recounted stories in his books from his childhood in the Provence. The author Jean Giono (1895-1970), born in Manosque, was emotionally very close to his heritage in the Provence; in his writings, he described the world of the mountain farmers. The writer and Nobel Prize winner Albert Camus (1913-1960) was born in Algiers and found a new home in Lourmarin; his grave is located in this city today. During the occupation, the English writer Samuel Beckett (1906-1990) hid in Roussillon. The astrologist Nostradamus, born in 1503 in St-Rémy-de-Provence, spent the last years of his life in Salon-de-Provence up until his death in 1566. In the small village of Sérignan-du-Comtat near Mont Ventoux, there once lived the most important insect researcher in France, Jean-Henri Fabre (1823-1915). The legendary orgies of Marquis de Sade (1740-1814), took place in his castle located in Lacoste.

Folklore

Those who enjoy traditional folklore will have ample opportunity to experience this in the Provence. The residents of this region lay emphasis on celebrating festivals and holidays in the traditional manner. On these occasions there are parades and dances with costumes and music typical of the Provence. Of course, over the years, these have taken on the character of tourist attractions but in more remote areas, the true origins can still be experienced.

→ *Entertainment, Holidays and Celebrations*

Fontaine-de-Vaucluse

Population: 650; elevation: 80 metres (262 feet)

Fontaine-de-Vaucluse is located around 30 kilometres (19 miles) east of Avignon and is accessible from Isle-sur-la-Sorgue via the D 25. It is best to park at one of the parking areas at the entrance to town and then explore this, the most heavily visited town in the Provence, on foot.

Fontaine-de-Vaucluse / **Sights**

The main attraction here is the spring which yields the most water in the world. It was already mentioned by Petrarca and discharges 150 cubic centimetres per second. However, it seems that this so-called spring is actually an underground river, which presumably is fed by the run-off and rain from the Plateaus of Vaucluse and Ventoux. The complex network of subterranean caves constantly attracts scientists, and since 1955, even the famous French oceanographer Jacques Cousteau. Above the spring in the cliffs are the ruins of the old fortress, offering a splendid view. The exhibition on caves on the way to the spring is the result of 30 years of research and includes minerals, stones and reproductions of landscapes and caves. One should not miss a visit to the Musée des Restrictions, exhibiting various objects documenting rationing in France during the two world wars and the war of 1870/71. Objects displayed here include ration coupons, bicycle tires made of cork, shoes with wooden soles etc. Unfortunately, this museum draws less attention, but this makes it all the more worth recommending since all of this was collected by Raymond Granier on his own initiative. Also very interesting is a visit to the paper mill Vallis Clausa. Here, paper is still made by hand using the same methods as in the 15th century. The paper pulp is comprised of scraps of fabric, flax, hemp and cotton and is mixed using the power from a moss-covered water wheel in the Sorgue. The shop offers a number of typical souvenirs but also has some practical objects like high-quality watercolour paper. The Petrarca Museum is dedicated to the famous citizen of this town, the Italian poet Francesco Petrarca (1304-1374). He took refuge in this town for sixteen years, the victim of his unrequited love for Laura, and wrote poetry. This museum displays a number of old edition of the poet's works. The St-Véran Church from the 11th century with Romanesque arches and classic columns houses the sarcophagus of the Bishop of Cavaillon from the 6th century in its crypt. Another interesting place to visit is the glass factory in which one can observe the glass blowers at work. Tours are free of charge, however, a small tip is appropriate. In the showroom articles can also be purchased.

Fontaine-de-Vaucluse / **Practical Information**

Accommodation

Hotels: ** La Gueulardière, 1 avenue J. Charmasson, Tel: (90) 38 10 52 and (90) 38 46 00, 19 rooms 110-230 FF.

Le Vieux Isle, 15 rue Danton, Tel: (90) 38 00 46, 10 rooms 100-130 FF.

Camping: ** Les Prés, Tel: (90) 20 32 38.

Youth Hostels: chemin de la Vignasse, Tel: (90) 20 31 65.

Restaurants: ** Parc, rue des Bourgades, Logis de France, (with 12 rooms 210 FF), Tel: (90) 20 31 57, terrace directly over the water, complete meals 105-216 FF.

** Host. du Château, waterfront location, Tel: (90) 20 31 54, complete meals 85-140 FF.

* Philip, Tel: (90) 20 31 81, at the base of the waterfalls, complete meals 85-190 FF.

Sports Facilities: The Sorgue offers excellent fishing. Spectators can observe how fish are dumped into the river just beyond the source to be caught by anglers within the city.

Important Addresses: Tourist information, place de l'Église, Tel: (90) 20 32 22.

Fontvieille

Population: 3,500; elevation: 20 metres (65 feet)

From Arles, one can drive to the town of Fontvieille via the D 17/D 33. Fontvieille is 10 kilometres (6¼ miles) from Arles. This city is closely related to the French author Alphonse Daudet (1840-1897). Somewhat outside of town at the end of the pine-lined Allée des Pins, is the small Daudet Museum, housed in a windmill. This is supposedly the location where the famous work "Letters from the Mill" was written. It is a nice notion if one disregards the fact that Daudet neither set foot in nor wrote a line in this mill — he visited Fontvieille only occasionally. The ground floor is decorated with memorabilia like manuscripts, books, caricatures and engravings.

Fontvieille / **Practical Information**

Accommodation

Hotels: *** La Regalido (Michel), offering good specialities, advance reservations are recommended, beautiful flower garden, Tel: (90) 54 60 22, 14 rooms 750-1200 FF, complete meals 210-390 FF.

** Valmajour, adjacent park, route d'Arles, Tel: (90) 54 62 33, 32 rooms 210-330 FF.
*** La Peiriero (without restaurant), avenue Baux, Tel: (90) 97 76 10, 40 rooms 300-500 FF.
** Mazets de Roches, 5.5 km (3½ miles) toward Tarascon via the D 33, Tel: (90) 91 34 89, modern accommodation, 24 rooms 400-540 FF, complete meals starting at 110 FF.
Camping: Camping Municipal des Pins, Tel: (90) 97 78 69.
Restaurants: * Le Homard, rue Nord, Tel: (90) 97 75 34, complete meals 85-185 FF.
* Laetitia, rue Lion, Tel: (90) 97 72 14, (with 9 rooms 110-165 FF), complete meals 65-95 FF.
Shopping: A market takes place on Mondays and Fridays.
Transportation : Buses operate daily to Arles, Salon, Aix, Marseille. Information is available by contacting Tel: (90) 96 27 64 or the tourist information offices.
Important Addresses: Tourist information, à l'Hôtel de Ville, Tel: (90) 97 70 01.

A typical scene in the Provence: the copious colours of the landscape

Fuel (Essence)

If driving a car with a catalytic converter in France, one need not worry: the supply of lead free fuel (essence sans plomb) is sufficient, although it is not available everywhere. Automobile clubs can usually provide a list of service stations offering lead-free fuel. Prices for one litre of fuel as of February 1991 are as follows:
Normal (90-91 octane): 5.04 FF (£ .51; $ .90)
Diesel: 3.50 FF (£ .36; $ .63)
Lead-free (95 octane): 4.80-5.47 FF (£ .48-.56; $ .85-.98)
Lead-free (98 octane): 4.85-5.50 FF (£ .49-.56; $ .86-.98)
Super (98 octane): 5.16 FF (£ .52;$ .92)
Some fuel pumps are automatic; these will only accept 10 FF coins. Fuel is duty free in canisters up to ten litres. With cars with catalytic converters, up to 100 litres are tolerated.

Geography

The true charm of the Provence lies in the diversity of its landscapes, which seems to be constantly changing: the Camargue with its fine sand and endless salt marshes; the white limestone range of Les Alpilles; the limestone massif of Ste-Victoire; the densely wooded Luberon mountain range; the fertile Vaucluse plain with its vineyards, vegetable fields and orchards and the plateau with its canyons, barren cliffs and towering Mont Ventoux. Numerous river systems, some dried up, can swell to overflowing during the spring run-off or after heavy rains. Canals dissect the plain and provide water for the extensive agricultural areas. Growing in the more barren regions are only more resistant species of plant life.
→*Vegetation*

Gigondas

Population: 700; elevation: 400 metres (1,308 feet)
Gigondas is located 16 kilometres (10 miles) southwest of Vaison-la-Romaine and is accessible via the D 977/D 7. This small town with the remnants of a city wall and a castle is famous for its red wines, which rank among the best in the Provence. Situated on the western slopes of the Dentelles de Montmirail, a mountain range west of Mont Ventoux, Gigondas makes a good starting point for hiking tours.
Worth seeing in this town are the ruins the walls surrounding a Château as well as the church from the 11th century.

Gigondas / Practical Information

Accommodation: ** Les Florets, 1.5 km (1 mile) from town, Tel: (90) 65 85 01, 15 rooms 225-260 FF, complete meals 110-170 FF.
About 6 km (three and three quarters miles) via D 7 and route Vacqueyras in Montmirail: ** Montmirail, Tel: (90) 65 84 01, modern accommodation, 46 rooms 255-400 FF, complete meals 110-200 FF.
Restaurants: ** Les Florets, route des Dentelles, Tel: (90) 65 85 01, complete meals start at 110 FF.
** Montmirail, par Vacqueyras, Tel: (90) 65 84 01, complete meals start at 130 FF.
Shopping: Wine, Amadieu Pierre, Rey André Domaine St André, Veyrat Pierre.
Sports Facilities: Mountain climbing school Club Alpin-Ecole d'Escalade, Café de la Poste, Tel: (90) 65 85 35; tennis courts; fishing in the nearby river Ouvèze; in the surrounding regions, there are four swimming pools; horseback riding at Centre Equèstre de Gigondas, Rout des Florets, Tel: (90) 65 00 91.
Transportation : There are bus routes to Carpentras.
Taxi: Tel: (90) 65 89 62.
Important Addresses
Office de Tourisme: Place du Portail, Tel: (90) 65 85 46.
Town Hall: Tel: (90) 65 86 90.
Gendarmerie/Police: Tel: (90) 62 94 08.
Fire Department: Tel: (90) 65 87 33.
Post Office: Tel: (90) 65 85 00.

Glanum / Les Antiques

Located amid a beautiful landscape with a view of Mont Ventoux and the Durance Valley is the heavily frequented tourist attraction of Glanum. It is situated 1 kilometre (a little over half a mile) south of St-Rémy on both sides of the D 5.

Glanum / **History**

The Gaelic-Ligurian settlement of Glanum — dating back to the 8th century B.C. — was engaged in active trading and commerce with the Greek city of Massalia (Marseille). With the passing of time, the Greeks settled into Glanum in the 3rd century B.C. and developed it into a flourishing commercial centre. The location on the roadway from Italy to Spain was influential in this development. Subsequently, the Romans (who had conquered the city of Massalia in the first century B.C. and continued their conquests from this base) encountered a prosperous and culturally developed city upon their arrival. The

Romans took over the role of the Greeks and built their typically impressive buildings. In this way, a construction boom took place under the rule of Augustus. Prosperity steadily increased up until the third century A.D. With the arrival of the Germanic Barbarians, Glanum sank into ruins. The survivors founded St-Rémy nearby. Although two monuments in this city were already known during the Middle Ages, archaeological excavations first began in Glanum in 1921. During the course of these excavations, archaeologists have uncovered only a small portion of this city; excavation work continues.

Glanum / **Sights**

When approaching from St-Rémy, the two Roman monuments Les Antiques are on the right-hand side of the road near the parking area. The construction of these dates back to the reign of Augustus (27 B.C. to 14 A.D.). The 18 metre (60 feet) high column-shaped monument was built as a memorial in honour of Augustus' two grandsons, Casius and Lucius, who fell in battle at an early age. Around the base of this well preserved monument are four reliefs depicting scenes from various battles. Above these are four columns with ornamented capitals. At the top is a type of round temple in which statues of both Casius and Lucius can be seen. It remains unknown whether the monument a few yards beyond the first is a city gate (Arc Municipal), a triumphal arch or a memorial structure. What is certain is that this is the oldest construction of its kind on French soil, dating back to 10 A.D. The reliefs on this gateway depict battle and capitulation scenes during the wars with the Gauls.

A few yards further on the opposite side of the road is the entrance to the ruins of Glanum (open 9 am to noon and 2 to 6 pm; October to April until 5 pm). At the entrance, one is given a small map providing an overview of the individual excavation sites at which, as previously mentioned, buildings from three different cultures have been uncovered. Directly at the entrance are the ruins of Roman living quarters with an inner courtyard and arcade, dating back to the 2nd century A.D. Adjacent to this are shops, the holy site of the Kybale, mosaic floors, thermal baths and the forum which was built on the ruins of a Greek house. Originating from the Greek period is the gateway constructed from massive blocks leading to the springs which was considered sacred by all three cultures. The terraces at the outer edge of the excavation site was a holy site for the Gaelic culture. Their origin is dated at 600 years B.C.

Gordes

Population: 1,600; elevation: 360 metres (1,177 feet)
The "white city" of Gordes is 17 kilometres (10½ miles) north of Cavaillon. Masses of tourists flock to this city each year. It is accessible via the D 2 and D 15.

Gordes / **Sights**

The mere appearance of this town is an attraction in and of itself. Laid out over a series of terraces, this city clings to the slopes and sparkles in the sunshine of the Provence. One should park at the parking area outside of the town in front of the Gendarmerie. This town has only a few stairways which are only accessible by foot. The main attraction of Gordes is the Renaissance castle from the 16th century: the artist Victor Vasarely (born in Hungary in 1908) rented this castle for the symbolic amount of 1 FF per year and restored it at his own expense, transforming it into a remarkable museum. His modern works coupled and contrasting with the historical surroundings is an excellent combination. It is not a museum in the conventional contemplative sense: the museum is set up didactically. At the press of a button the scenes in the showcases begin to move, "animating" works from a given period. On the ground floor one can purchase lithographs, catalogues and slides of Vasarely's works — an enterprising artist! With the exception of Tuesdays, the castle is open from 10 am to noon and 2 to 6 pm, Tel: (90) 72 02 89. Another museum dedicated to the works of this artist is the Fondation Vasarely in → *Aix-en-Provence.* In the St-Firmin Church (built at the beginning of the 18th century) are a number of interesting → *votive pictures.* The cemetery (on a cul-de-sac behind the post office) is a reminder of the tragic history of this city: at the end of the Second World War, the citizens of Gordes were denounced by the Gestapo. Gordes was attacked and, for the most part, destroyed. Many of the residents were killed. Before entering the town, there is a small Roman Museum, the Inslula Maria, a reconstructed Roman villa with frescoes and mosaics as well as a small collection of archaeological finds. A unique outdoor museum is located 3.5 kilometres (2 miles) outside of Gordes: the village of Bories (Village des Bories). Here, a village has been reconstructed, offering a glimpse into the past centuries *(→Bories).* For those interested in art, there is a museum which can be highly recommended around 5 kilometres (3 miles) outside of Gordes: the Musée du Vitrail (Glass Museum) founded by the artist Frédérique Duran. Beautifully located in a park, on display here are Duran's highly individual stained glass windows. The museum offers insight into the production of glass and the art of stained glass, including numerous old objects and tools. In the large country house within the park is a further attraction, the Moulin des Bouillons, an antique oil mill from the 16th century (open 10 am to noon and 2 to 7 pm, during the summer to 7 pm; in winter, open only on Saturdays, Sundays and holidays).

Gordes / **Practical Information**

Accommodation

Hotels: *** Domaine de l'Enclos, route de Sénanque, Tel: (90) 72 08 22, modern accommodation, especially attractive through its park and view of the Luberon range, 5 rooms 860-1260 FF, complete meals from 220 FF.
** La Mayanelle, Rue de la Combe, Tel: (90) 72 00 28, nicely furnished, 10 rooms 200-300 FF, complete meals 130-190 FF.
** Le Gordos (without restaurant), route de Cavaillon, 1.5 km (1 mile outside of town, Tel: (90) 72 00 75, 15 rooms 275-340 FF.
* Auberge de Carcarille, Les Gervais, Logis de France, 2.5 km (1½ miles) via the D 2, Tel: (90) 72 02 63, 11 rooms 210-250 FF, complete meals 80-150 FF.
Camping: *** Les Sources, Tel: (90) 72 12 48.

Automobile Repair: Peugeot-Talbot Garage JPC, Tel: (90) 72 00 24.

Medical Care: There are two physicians in town, Tel: (90) 72 00 48, one dentist and a pharmacy.

Restaurants: *** Les Bories, 2 km (1¼ miles) from town via route de Sénanque, Tel: (90) 72 00 51 (with 7 rooms 450-600 FF), filled with works of art from Bories, serving good specialities, reservations are recommended, complete meals 265-400 FF.

Shopping: The market takes place every Tuesday in the centre of town in the area around the castle; it has been adapted to tourism, offering souvenirs in a picturesque atmosphere. If purchasing honey in town, the Peyron store is recommended (also offering lavender products). In the Soleiado shop, there are high-quality, although rather expensive, fabrics typical for the Provence, available by the metre or already made into blouses, skirts, table linens, scarves or handbags.

Sports Facilities: Riding School/Hotel Centre équestre des Luquets, Anne Duriau, Tel: (90) 72 07 97.

Important Addresses

Tourist Information: Place du Château, Tel: (90) 72 02 75.
Gendarmerie/Police: Tel: (90) 72 01 01.

Goult

Population: 1,050

Halfway between Cavaillon and Apt on the N 100, the D 105 leads from Notre-Dame de Lumière up to the small remote town of Goult. The d'Agoult family, who once resided in the castle, gave the town its name. Earlier in the 12th and 13th centuries, Goult was an important town for the art of glass-blowing. Today, a number of artists have settled here, predominantly potters.

Goult / **Sights**

On Rue de la République (one can park here at one of the large parking areas) there is a massive parish church from the 12th century. Narrow streets lead uphill past the idyllic houses and squares to the château from the 17th century. The portions which have been preserved over the years have been renovated, and this is now under private ownership. From a small observation area, one will have a beautiful view of the Vaucluse Valley.

Goult / **Practical Information**

Medical Care: In addition to two physicians and one dentist, there is a pharmacy

Restaurants: Le Tonneau, Tel: (90) 72 22 35.

Shopping: Wine, Cave Coopérative Maubert Bernard "La Verrière."

Sports Facilities: Horseback riding, Mas de la Barbe, horse training school, Patrice Gondange, Tel: (90) 72 32 76.

Herbs and Spices

Those who enjoy cooking will know what to look for at the marketplaces in the Provence. These offer an abundance of dried herbs and spices and even those less versed in the arts of gourmet cooking will enjoy the symphony of aromas in the Provence.

Romarin	Rosemary
Thym	Thyme (garden variety)
Serpolet	Wild Thyme
Majolaine	Marjoram
Sauge	Sage
Origan	Oregano
Basilic	Basil
Cerfeuil	Chervil
Genièvre	Juniper Berries
Lavande	Lavender

Laurier	Bay Leaf
Sel	Salt
Poivre	Pepper
Cumin	Cumin
Cannelle	Cinnamon
Aneth	Dill
Fenouil	Fennel
Persil	Parsley
Civette, Coboulette	Chives
Macis	Mace
Melange Salades	Salad Herbs
Melange Poissons	Mixed Herbs for Fish
Herbes de Provence	Herbs of the Provence

The last in the above list is a mixture with no set composition. It is usually a mixture of rosemary, thyme and oregano (among other herbs and spices). As a general rule, the freshly picked and dried herbs in season are used.

The intense gold an yellow of the fields an a view of Goult, the secluded artists' village

Everyone who enjoys cooking can compose their own mixture — the combinations are limitless.

History and Politics

The first evidenced settlement in the Provence was that of the Ligurians around 1500 B.C. Around 1000 B.C., an increasing number of Celts (Gauls) arrived and there was more or less a peaceful coexistence among the cultures. In cultural history, one speaks of a Celto-Ligurian Epoch. Southern France gained historical significance around 600 B.C. when the Greeks arrived from Asia Minor, landing on the coast of what is now Marseille. In cooperation with the Ligurians, they expanded the city of Massalia *(→Marseille)*. This coexistence continued quite peacefully and trade developed between the two cultures. In addition to Massalia, the Greeks founded other commercial bases along the coast, the largest of which were Antipolis (Antibes) and Nikaea (Nice). From these points, they made the inhabitants acquainted with the cultivation of fig trees, olive trees and grapes. This peaceful development was abruptly halted with the attacks of the Carthaginians (from 542 B.C.) who subsequently occupied Massalia for decades. With the withdrawal of the Carthaginians came the increasingly frequent Celtic attacks. Feeling threatened, Massalia requested assistance from Rome around 126 B.C. Rome was quite willing to help and decisively defeated the Celts in 123 B.C. To secure their power, the Romans built the fortress of Aquae Sextiae a year later near the former Gaelic stronghold, which was later to become *→Aix-en-Provence.* Meanwhile, Rome continued in its conquest of further regions, falling into conflict with the Germanic tribes. The last significant battles took place in 102 B.C. when Marius devastatingly defeated the Teutons near Aquae Sextiae and in 52 B.C. when the last uprising under the rule of Vercingetroix was violently quashed. The Roman province of Provincia Gallia Narbonensis first flourished during the rule of Augustus around 1 B.C./1 A.D. Construction activity was incredible. The evidence of this can still be seen today in Vaison-la-Romaine, Orange, Nîmes and Arles. The main roadways Via Domitia, Via Agrippa and the coastal Via Aurelia, were expanded, connecting the Provence with the Roman Empire. After the reign of Constantine (306-337) important for the Provence and its Christianisation, more and more flaws became apparent in the Roman Empire. The Visigoths followed by the Burgundi, Vandals and Ostrogoths increasingly penetrated the southern regions. The fall of the Roman Empire was sealed in 476 A.D. The fate of the Provence was uncertain and after some confusion it fell under the rule of the Franconians in 530 A.D. However, peace and normalcy were not to result. The land was increasingly invaded by Moors or Saracens, who were able to maintain control over portions of the Provence up to the 10th century. After the death of Charlemagne and the subsequent division of France into three parts (843 A.D.), the Provence came under the rule of the King of Burgundy. Resulting from an succession agreement in year 1033, Burgundy and the Provence became a part of the Holy Roman Empire. Owing to distances involved alone the Provence and its larger cities enjoyed relative independence. The Count of Toulouse acted as governor, to be followed by the Count of Barcelona. In 1246, the Provence came under the control of Charles of Anjou, the brother of the French King Louis IX. This was the result of the marriage of the Count of Barcelona's daughter. René, the successor from the house of Anjou and also called the "good king," was a true blessing for the Provence *(→Aix-en-Provence).* His successor, Charles of Maine awarded control over the Provence to the French King Louis XI, with the exception of Avignon and Comtat Venaissin, regions which belonged to the popes up until 1790. Established by Louis XII in 1501, the parliament of Aix, which also served as a court of justice, was originally obliging to the king *(→Religion)* but did increasingly act on behalf of the interests of the Provence so that in the 16th century, the Provence was granted a type of self-administration. In 1539, French was declared the official language. During the counter-reformation in the 16th century, Charles V's troops fought against the French King Francis I and occupied portions of the Provence. The rest of the 16th and the 17 century were overshadowed by the religious wars. The unified nation with the central government in Paris, created by Richelieu and Louis XIV, rang in the era of absolutism. Southern France was increasingly disadvantaged and the cities came more and more into conflict with Richelieu in their ambition for freedom and independence. This prompted Richelieu to raze one fortress after the other during battles lasting for years. The epidemic of the plague in 1720 claimed over 100,000 lives in the Provence alone. The French Revolution in 1789 swept away the decadent system of absolutism. The Count of Mirabeau, also the son of Proveçal nobility, appeared on the revolutionary scene. As president of the National Assembly, he represented a moderate political course; his untimely death (1749-1791) hindered him in preventing the radicalisation of the revolution, which met with resistance in the Provence. More and more frequently, Paris sent so-called penal expeditions to the rebellious cities. Resulting from the division of France into individual départements governed centrally from Paris, the Provence lost its independent role. For decades it took on a "provincial" role. Neither the restored empire nor the subsequent bourgeois government took interest in the economic development of southern France. The First World War left the

Provence virtually untouched; this cannot be claimed of the Second World War with the German occupation (1942-1944) and the arrival of the allied forces in 1944. Scars from the Nazi regime can be found everywhere in the towns and reminders on the gravestones in the cemeteries. In the 1950's the central government took interest in developing the Provence as an industrial area. The development was promoted by the increase in tourism, which began in the 19th century with the English on the Côte d'Azur. The Fourth Republic, established in 1946 was replaced in 1958 by the Fifth Republic headed by Charles de Gaulle, who influenced the development of French politics for 11 years as president. His successor in 1969 was Pompidou. During his term in office, Pompidou consolidated the 95 Départements established during the French Revolution. After Pompidou's death in 1974, Giscard d'Estaing took over the government. In the presidential election of 1981, the socialist Mitterand was able to capture the majority of votes and became president of France. The parliamentary election two months later brought the Socialists the majority in the National Assembly, which they later lost to the conservatives in 1986. Jacques Chirac became the governmental leader. A time of the "cohabitation" of a socialist president and a Gaullist prime minister began. In 1988, François Mitterand was reelected to the presidency, and the Parti socialiste was able to secure a narrow majority in the new elections.

→*Economy, Religion*

Holidays and Celebrations

Legal Holidays in France: January 1, Easter Monday, May 1, May 8 (Armistice Treaty, 1945), Christ's Ascension, Pentecost Monday, July 14 (National Holiday/Bastille Day 1789), August 15 (Mary's Ascension), November 1 (All Saints' Day), November 11 (Armistice Treaty, 1918), December 25.

Additional Celebrations

Easter/Arles: Feria, bullfights (Spanish)

Last Sunday in April/Arles: Festival of the Gardians (cattle herders): mass; ceremonial blessing of the horses; bullfights

24/25 May: Gypsy pilgrimage in Les Stes-Maries-de-la-Mer

Pentecost/Apt: Parade on horseback; music festival

1 June/Boulbon: wine procession with the ceremonial blessing of the wine

23 June:/Valréas: Festival of Petit St-Jean

First Monday in July/Arles: Bullfights à la Provence

14 July/Tarascon: Arrival of the steers

Mid-July/Le Baux: Dance Festival

Mid-July/Carpentras: Festival of Notre-Dame-de-Santé and the nightly procession
Last Sunday in July/Apt: Pilgrimage to Saint Anne
15-17 August/Roussillon: Ochre Festival
24 December/Les Baux: Shepherds' Christmas, midnight mass
In addition to these, there is an abundance of festivals of every kind. The people of the Provence love this form of diversion and almost every town or village will have their own celebrations — whether classical or folk music festivals, festivals for agricultural produce or traditional religious pilgrimages. What is important is that these offer the chance to meet, celebrate, dance and sing — and of course to enjoy the products of the grape harvest. Since these festivals are a factor of growing importance for the regional economy, tourist offices try to attract visitors. Excellent informational materials are available all over the Provence
→*Tourist Information under individual entries*

Hospitals (hôpital)

There is a hospital in every larger city. Before starting one's journey, it is a good idea to check one's health insurance coverage in a foreign country and to complement the coverage with a supplemental travel health insurance policy if necessary.
→*Medical Care*

Insurance

In addition to liability insurance for an automobile, if driving in France, normal liability and health insurance is usually sufficient in France. It is advisable to contact one's insurance agent to check on coverage abroad. In addition, one can of course supplement insurance coverage during the duration of the holiday by taking out short-term policies like, for instance, baggage insurance.
→*Medical Care, Travel Documents*

International Press

The Provence is mainly a holiday destination in France; therefore international newspapers can commonly be found in the larger cities such as Avignon, Arles, Aix and Marseille. However, these often arrive one day later. Even if one can only speak a few phrases of French, one should still take the time to look through some of the local newspapers (Les Provençal, Le Soir, Dauphiné, Libéré, La Marseillaise, Le Méridional-La France). This is worthwhile for the local reports and advertisements.

Joucas

Population: 200; elevation: 265 metres (867 feet)

To reach Joucas, one must turn off of the D2 onto the D 102, six kilometres (almost four miles) northeast of Gordes.

Joucas is a picturesque town on the slope of the Plateau de Vaucluse which has been discovered by a number of artists. Still the town has not lost its character typical of the Provence.

Accommodation: *** Mas des Herbes Blanches, 2.5 kilometres (1½ miles) on the D 102A route de Murs, Tel: (90) 05 79 79, modern accommodation with a beautiful view of the Luberon range, 16 rooms 670-1150 FF, complete meals 260-370 FF.

*** Phébus, route de Murs, Tel: (90) 05 78 83, modern accommodation, 16 rooms 580-690 FF, complete meals 190-390 FF.

* Hostellerie des Commandeurs, Logis de France, Tel: (90) 05 78 01, 14 rooms 140-190 FF, complete meals 80-130 FF.

Sports Facilities: Horseback riding (with hotel) Mas du Buis, Monsieur Herbst, Tel: (90) 72 02 22, offering room and board.

Julien Bridge (Pont Julien)

About 7 kilometres west of Apt on the N 100, there is a sign for Pont Julien, a Roman bridge spanning the Coulon River. This bridge was built in the 1st century A.D. and is still so well preserved today that it can accommodate modern automobile traffic. However, if one descends the riverbanks, one will wonder just how much longer this 2,000 year old bridge will withstand the pollution. The Coulon River is a cesspit used for draining chemical waste.

La Barben

Population: 350; elevation: 114 metres (373 feet)

La Barben is located 8 kilometres (5 miles) south of Salon-de-Provence.

The former fortress, built in the 12th century and changed ownership many times (King René among others), and was transformed into a castle in the 17th century, without losing its fortress character. Worth seeing are the terraces, from which one has a beautiful view of the Alpilles. Also worthwhile is a look around the interior of the castle with its tapestries from the 16th and 17th centuries (open 10 am to noon and 2 to 4 pm, until 5 pm during low season). The 30 hectare large (75 acre) park surrounding the castle is now a zoo without cages, an aquarium and a bird house (open from 10 am to noon and 1:30 to 6 pm or until sunset).

Restaurant: ** Touloubre (with 7 rooms from 240 FF), Pélissanne, Tel: (90) 55 16 85, complete meals 117-230 FF.

Lacoste

Population: 300; elevation: 326 metres (1,066 feet)
Lacoste, 14 kilometres (9 miles) southwest of Apt, is a small village which is closely related to the Marquis de Sade (1740-1814). De Sade celebrated orgies here in his castle, which he described in his works "Justine" and "120 days of Sodom." The castle from the 16th century in the upper portion of the village was looted and destroyed in 1792. Today, the ruins have been partially restored and can be toured; however, only with the permission of the present owner. Also worth seeing is the Romanesque church from the 12th century as are the ruins of the city wall and a bell tower.

Lagnes

From the N 100, about halfway between Coustellet and L'Isle-sur-la-Sorgue, the D 186 leads to Lagnes.
Camping: ** Camping La Coutelière, route de Fontaine, Tel: (90) 20 33 97.

Language Guide

It is certainly advantageous to have at least a basic command of the French language when travelling to the Provence. This also provides the opportunity to have a more in-depth conversation with local residents. The residents of the Provence do, however, tend to talk quite quickly.
The following is a brief introduction to the French language. It, of course, could never be a substitute for a language course, since the pronunciation requires a certain amount of practice. However, do not be shy if your French is only basic: the French will be very accommodating and patient.

Good morning/day!	Bonjour!
Good evening!	Bonsoir!
Good night!	Bonne nuit!
See you soon!	à bientôt!
Until tomorrow!	à demain!
Good-bye!	Au revoir!
Good luck! Best wishes!	Bonne chance!
Mister	Monsieur
Mrs./Miss	Madame/Mademoiselle
Ladies and Gentlemen!	Mesdames et Messieurs!
Doctor	Monsieur le Docteur

In France, it is considered impolite to answer with only "yes" or "no" or to say only "Bonjour" or "Bonsoir." It is more polite to add "Monsieur," "Madame" or "Mademoiselle."

Pleased to meet you!	Enchanté!
How are you?	Ça va?
(very) well, thank you!	(assez) bien, merci!
thank you very much!	merci beaucoup!
My name is ...	Mon nom est ...
This is ...	C'est ...
my husband/son/boyfriend	mon mari/fils/ami
my wife/daughter/girlfriend	ma femme/Fille/mon amie
yes, no	oui, non
please	s'il vous plaît
you're welcome	de rien
thank you very much	merci beaucoup
very good!	très bien!
That's right!	C'est ça!
Okay!	D'accord!
never	jamais
nothing	rien
No, thank you.	Non, merci.
I can't (don't want to).	Je ne veux (peux) pas.
maybe	peut-être
Excuse me please!	Excusez, s'il vous plaît!
I'm sorry	Pardon!
I don't understand	je ne comprends pas
Do you speak English?	Parlez-vous anglais
why, what, who	pourquoi, que, qui
which ...?	quel (quelle) ...?
to whom, with whom	à qui, avec qui
what?	comment?
where, from where,	où, d'où
where is ...?	où est ...?
how many	combien
how long?	combien de temps?
when	quand
at what time?	à quelle heure?
It is already late.	Il est déjà tard.

today	aujourd'hui
yesterday	hier
tomorrow	demain
morning	le matin
noon	à midi
afternoon	l'après-midi
evening	le soir
second, minute, hour	seconde, minute, heure
day, week, month, year	jour, semaine, mois, an (année)
Monday, Tuesday, Wednesday	lundi, mardi, mercredi
Thursday, Friday, Saturday	jeudi, vendredi, samedi
Sunday	dimanche
spring, summer	printemps, été
autumn, winter	automne, hiver
weather	temps
right, left	à droite, à gauche
north, south	nord, sud
east, west	est, ouest
That will be all!	c'est tout!
large, small	grand, petit
price	prix
(too) expensive	(trop) cher
many/a lot, a little	beaucoup, un peu
How much does ... cost?	quel est le prix de ...?
more, less	plus, moins
Do you have ...?	Avez-vous ...?
May I ...?	Puis-je ...?
What would you like?	Que désirez-vous?
What is that?	Qu'est-ce que c'est?
Who is it?	Qui et là?
What is ... called?	Comment s'appelle ...?
What is your name?	Qui est votre nom?
Please give me ...	Donnez-moi ..., s'il vous plaît
Please tell me ...	Dites-moi, s'il vous plaît, ...
I need ...	J'ai besoin de ...
open, closed	ouvert, fermé
Help!	Au secours!
police, accident	police, accident
doctor, ambulance	médecin, ambulance

0 zéro	10 dix	20 vingt
1 un	11 onze	21 vingt et un
2 deux	12 douze	22 vingt-deux
3 trois	13 treize	30 trente
4 quatre	14 quatorze	31 trente et un
5 cinq	15 quinze	40 quarante
6 six	16 seize	50 cinquante
7 sept	17 dix-sept	60 soixante
8 huit	18 dix-huit	70 soixante-dix
9 neuf	19 dix-neuf	71 soixante et onze
72 soixante-douze	80 quatre-vingts	90 quatre-vingt-dix
100 cent	101 cent un	110 cent dix
200 deux cent	1000 mille	2000 deux mille
1,000,000 un million		

Lauris

Population: 1,750; elevation: 82 metres (268 feet)
Lauris is located on the D 973 about 23 kilometres (15 miles) south of Apt. This town has a castle from the 18th century and a church from the 17th century.

Lauris / **Practical Information**

Accommodation: ** La Chaumière, Tel: (90) 08 20 25, with a view of the Durance Valley, 15 rooms 290-380 FF, complete meals 185-315 FF.
Automobile Repair: Citroën.
Medical Care: Physician and dentist; Pharmacy: rue Louis Mourre.
Restaurants: Wine coopérative.
Shopping: The market takes place on Mondays.
Sports Facilities: Two tennis courts.
Transportation: Bus routes to Avignon and Cavaillon.
Important Addresses
Tourist Information: Place de l'Eglise.
Gendarmerie/Police: in Cadenet, Tel: (90) 68 00 17.
Fire Department: Tel: (90) 68 01 25.
Town Hall: Tel: (90) 68 00 46 and (90) 68 05 09.

Les-Grau-du-Roi →*Camargue*

Les Baux-de-Provence

Population: 430; elevation: 280 metres (916 feet)

Even when approaching on the D 27 from St-Rémy-de Provence, the view of this 900 metre (2,943 feet) long and 200 metre (654 feet) wide block of stone with the remnants of a medieval fortress on top of it is very impressive. The houses and buildings in the town of Les Beaux, perched on the slopes below are in part restored and house numerous shops for tourists. Unfortunately, Les Beaux is overrun during the tourist season.

Les Baux / **History**

The fortress was the primary residence of the Lords of Les Beaux, who owned a number of scattered fortresses and villages during the Middle Ages. Around 1300, the fort attracted countless Troubadours from far away for the minstrel competition. At this legendary "court of the Troubadours," the singers competed for the favours of the noble ladies, whose tribunal decided which Troubadour was to receive the wreath and a kiss as the prize. An end was to be put to this idyll with the appearance of Raymund of Turenne, who was to inherit the rule of Les Baux in 1372. The surrounding villages suffered under the numerous brutal attacks by the new Lord of Baux. He is said to have cast prisoners from the cliffs for his mere pleasure. The writer Niebelschütz describes this in his novel "The Children of Darkness." To put an end to this gruesome acts, the king of France, the pope and the Count of the Provence joined forces, initiating a successful campaign against Les Baux. Raymund of Turenne drowned in the Rhône near Tarascon during his flight. The fort was razed and stripped of all importance. Only during the Reformation under the rule of the Count of Manville would Les Baux flourish once more, albeit only for a short time: as Les Baux developed into a Protestant refuge, the town was attacked and completely destroyed by Richelieu in 1632. The residents abandoned the ruins and only the streams of tourists which pour into Les Baux each year would bring life back into this town. The town is presently owned by Grimaldi of Monaco.

Les Baux / **Sights**

Les Baux is not accessible by car. Parking areas can be found at the entrance to the town, where one can also obtain a small map for orientation. The village is very picturesque with its old houses — if one can ignore the legions of tourists. Alleyways lead up the slopes to the main attraction of the village: past a former road-house from the 17th century displaying a Santons exhibition *(→Santons)* to the Eyguières Gate, which was formerly the entrance to the village. In the Hôtel des Porcelets, a municipal palace from the 16th century is the Museum for Contemporary Art, displaying works by Gleizes, Carzou, Buffet, Brayer and others. On Place St-Vincent is the chapel with white penitent benches from the 17th century, the Chapelle des Pénitents blancs. In this chapel are paintings by Yves Brayer. Also on Place St-Vincent is the St-Vincent Church from the 12th century. Every year, the famous Christmas mass of Les Baux takes place here — a 400 year old tradition. The Hôtel de Manville, a palais from the 16th century, houses the town hall and the Office de Tourisme today. Upon entering this old village of ruins, one will automatically enter the museum displaying archaeological finds of this region. During the past century, Bauxite was discovered in this area, giving the village its name. Touring the village does present certain dangers. One should definitely wear appropriate shoes. After crossing the extensive plateau, past an old cemetery, one will come upon an area offering a magnificent view of Arles, the Crau and Camargue. On clear days, one can even see all the way to the coast. At the edge of this plateau is a monument in honour of the Provençal poet Charloun Rieu (1846-1924). The tour leads by the Tour Sarrasine. Only those completely immune to a fear of heights should climb the old, worn and steep stone stairway, sometimes with only an iron bar as a railing. Still, the view from this point is worth the effort. Past the Chapelle Sainte-Cathérine, restored in the 16th century, one will come to the massive fortress ruins, surrounded by the ruins of the village. Those who still have enough time can see the famous Pavillon de la Reine Jeanne on a hike through the La Fontaine Valley. Queen Jeanne, the second wife of King René, did, however, live 100 years before its construction in 1581. About 500 metres (about ¼ mile) north of Les Baux on the D 27 in Val d'enfer is yet another impressive attraction: the Cathédrale d'Images (Cathedral of Pictures). In a quarry which had been abandoned for a hundred years, Albert Plécy (1914-1977) found that for which he had been searching: the "ultimate picture." The high, smooth and partially shadowed limestone walls form a colossal, three-dimensional canvas, on which coloured lights are projected and accompanied by synthesizer. The programme changes every season. Continual performances from March 15 to November 11, daily from 10 am to 7 pm; beginning in October only until 6 pm and closed Tuesdays (performances last around 30 minutes). Please note: the temperature inside is only a chilly 60 °F (15 °C).

Les Baux / **Practical Information**

Accommodation

Hotel: Bautezar, grande rue Frédéric Mistral, Tel: (90) 54 32 09, 10 rooms * Hostellerie de la Reine Jeanne, Tel: (90) 97 32 06, 11 rooms from 175 FF. *Camping:* In Maussane (4 km/2½ miles from Les Baux), Camping les Romarins, Tel: (90) 54 33 60.

Restaurants: In the valley are three exquisite restaurants (Les Baux is a tip for the gourmet) ***** Oustaù de Baumanière (Thuilier), with 13 rooms 725-820 FF, old residence with elegance, terrace decorated with flowers and numerous sports facilities, Tel: (90) 54 33 07, complete meals 350-500 FF.

*** La Riboto de Taven (beautiful terrace with a flower garden at the base of the cliff), Tel: (90) 97 34 23, complete meals 240-500 FF.

*** La Cabro d'Or, attractive and modern, with a shady terrace, a flower garden and pond, also has 22 rooms 420-640 FF, Tel: (90) 54 33 21, complete meals 250-370 FF.

In the extensive, secluded landscape of the Provence, one will often come upon these typical stone cottages

Shopping: The numerous shops offer everything from tacky souvenirs to typical specialities of the Provence and woven handicrafts (Les Olivades fabrics etc., Santons, pottery). The prices, however, are sometimes rather high. Most of this can be purchased more inexpensively elsewhere in the Provence, however not in such a spectacular setting.
Transportation: There are S.N.C.F. bus routes to Arles and Saint-Rémy, which, however, operate only sporadically outside of the tourist season.
Important Addresses: Office de Tourisme at the cul-de-sac near the castle, Tel: (90) 97 34 39.
The post office is located near the entrance to town.

Les Taillades

Located approximately 5 kilometres (3 miles) east of Cavaillon, Les Taillades is on the D 31. The D 143 then leads into town.

Les Taillades / **Sights**

The D 31 leads into the fertile plain on the Canal de Carpentras. The water in this canal is used to turn the water wheel which formerly belonged to the flour factory. A little further, one turns off onto the D 143, leading through Taillades into the Luberon mountains. At the bend in the road, a cul-de-sac branches off. This leads to a massive medieval fortress. On an elevation is a small church, which, like the other buildings, has been restored and is now under private ownership. The residents can certainly be envied. From here, there is a fantastic view of the Vaucluse plain with Cavaillon to the left.

Les Taillades / **Practical Information**

Shopping: A market takes place on Tuesdays.
Sports Facilities: Excursions on Horseback/Hotel Ranch El Dorado, Michel Vicini, route de Cavaillon, Tel: (90) 71 03 04.
Transportation: Taxi, Tel: (90) 78 39 39.

L'Isle-sur-la-Sorgue

Population: 13,000; elevation: 59 metres (193 feet)
L'Isle-sur-la-Sorgue is located some 10 kilometres (6¼ miles) north of Cavaillon on the D 938/N 100.
This "water city" is surrounded and dissected by five arms of the Sorgue. The inner city is accessible using one of the numerous bridges. In addition to the bridges, tree-lined boulevards and moss covered water wheels make up the

profile of this city. The water wheels are remnants from the Middle Ages, when they provided power to various manufacturers of paper and oil as well as flour mills and dyeworks. Today, they turn only for the tourists. Another attraction is the Sunday market which extends from the banks of the Sorgue into the inner city. Sold here is everything from antiques to fruits and vegetables, textiles, books and live animals.

L'Isle-sur-la-Sorgue / **Sights**

The church in the inner city was built during the 17th century, incorporating the former Gothic chapel. Upon entering the church, the Baroque atmosphere is almost stifling. Twenty-six gold angels on a blue background decorate the wall at the west portal. Carved wooden panels, statues of saints and numerous oil paintings embellish the interior. The main altar has a massive altar-piece. All of this uses the bright colours reminiscent of the Italian Baroque period. On the Place de la Juiverie stands the Hôtel-Dieu (hospital), which was built during the mid 18th century. Use the entrance on Rue Jean-Théophile. Tours are offered from June to September, offering better understanding of the chapel, the stairway with valuable wrought-iron landings from the 18th century and the pharmacy which is beautifully furnished and includes numerous containers and Fayence pottery.

L'Isle-sur-la-Sorgue / **Practical Information**

Accommodation

Hotels: ** Araxe H. (without restaurant), 1.5 km (1 mile) via the N 100 heading toward Apt, Tel: (90) 38 40 00, 34 rooms 270-330 FF.

** Les Névons (without restaurant), Chemin de Névons, Tel: (90) 20 72 00, 26 rooms 240-300 FF.

** Host. La Grangette "in the country," 6 km (about 4 miles) north on the D 938, Tel: (90) 20 00 77, 17 rooms 330-610 FF, complete meals 139-375 FF.

Camping: *** Municipal La Sorguette, Tel: (90) 38 05 71.

Automobile Repair: Citroën, Peugeot-Talbot, Renault.

Entertainment: Cinema, Tel: (90) 20 74 97.

Medical Care: The tourist information office, the police or one of the pharmacies mentioned will be able to recommend physicians. Ambulance, Tel: (90) 38 12 69.

Restaurants: ** Rascasse d'Argent, 4 km (2½ miles) via the D 25 on route Fontaine-de-Vaucluse, Tel: (90) 20 33 52, complete meals 61-163 FF.

Shopping: The market takes place on Tuesdays and Sundays, Sundays is the more extensive of the two (lasting until noon) with a very good antiques market, which is also open during the afternoon. In addition, the area offers a wide spectrum of shops.
Sports Facilities: Poney-Club de la Cathérine, Cathérine and Gérard Malen, chemin du Lagnien — route de Fontaine-de-Vaucluse, Tel: (90) 38 16 13, riding school/hotel; swimming pool is accessible via the avenue Bonaparte; tennis courts; fishing.
Transportation: Taxi, Tel: (90) 38 27 84.
Important Addresses
Office de Tourisme: place Église, Tel: (90) 38 04 78.
Town Hall: rue Carnot, Tel: (90) 38 06 45.
Gendarmerie/Police: cours Emile-Zola, Tel: (90) 38 00 17.
Fire Department: Caserne route de Velleron, Tel: (90) 38 03 40.
Post Office: quai Jean-Jaurès, Tel: (90) 38 12 90.

Lourmarin

Population: approximately 850; elevation: 230 metres (753 feet)
Lourmarin is situated about 5 km (3 miles) north of Cadenet (via the D 943). This is where the Nobel prize winner Albert Camus (1913-1960; born in Algeria) spent his last years. His grave can be found in the village cemetery.

Lourmarin / **Sights**

The castle at the entrance to the city (15th/16th century with Renaissance embellishments, fireplaces and a hexagonal tower) is now a meeting place for artists and scholarship recipients of the Academy of Art; Tel: (90) 68 15 23, open from 9 to 11:45 am and 2:30 to 6:15 pm (October 1 to June 30 until 5:45 pm), closed Tuesdays from November 1 to March 31. It is best to park one's car at the parking area near the castle outside of the city and continue to the city on foot. Albert Camus' residence in the Albert-Camus street no. 5 is not open to the public.

Lourmarin / **Practical Information**

Accommodation
Hotel: ** Guilles, modern accommodation, route Vaugines, 1.5 km (1 mile) via the D 56, Tel: (90) 68 30 55, 28 rooms 280-470 FF, snacks 85-130 FF.
Camping: *** Camping Les Hautes Prairies, Route de Vaugines (600 sites), Tel: (90) 68 02 81.

Medical Care: Pharmacy, avenue Philippe de Girard, Tel: (90) 68 20 25.
Restaurants: ** Restaurant Ollier, place Fontaine, Tel: (90) 68 02 03, complete meals 135-255 FF.
Coopérative Vinicole Barthélemy, Tel: (90) 68 02 18.
Important Addresses:
Post Office: avenue Philippe de Girard, Tel: (90) 68 04 14.
Town Hall: Tel: (90) 68 04 13.

Luberon

The wooded limestone Luberon mountain range extends from east to west between Cavaillon and Manosque. At the extremities of this range are Durance and the Coulon Valley. The Combe de Lourmarin, a narrow valley, divides the Luberon into the major and minor range. The northern portion is more rugged, untamed and more barren, while the southern portion is characterised more frequently by lush vegetation. A portion of the Luberon (100,000 hectares/250,000 acres) was made into a nature reserve (Parc Naturel Regional du Luberon) in 1977. This is an excellent area for hiking. The Côte-du-Luberon wines enjoy a very good reputation.

Maillane

Population: approximately 1,500
Maillane is located about seven kilometres (4¼ miles) northwest of St-Rémy-de-Provence on the D 5.
The author and Nobel Prize winner Frédéric Mistral was born in 1830 in Maillane, the son of a wealthy farmer. Throughout his life he remained in this town. The house where he lived up until his death in 1914 has remained unchanged and is open to the public (Musée Mistral). Mistral's final resting place is in the cemetery in a mausoleum which he designed himself.
Restaurant: ** Oustalet Maïanen, Tel: (90) 95 74 60, complete meals 100-160 FF.

Maps

The ign map (1:25,000/1 kilometre = 4 cm) is available covering portions of the Provence, e.g. Cavaillon, eastern Apt with Roussillon and Bonnieux, Carpentras etc. — the most detailed map where virtually every building and every fountain is included; ign Carte Touristique (1:100,000/1 km = 1 cm) No. 67 =

As if captured by an artist's brush: a still life in a small mountain village in the Provence ▶

La Mandragoule

Marseilles, Carpentras etc., No. 66 = Camargue; Michelin (1:200,000/220 km = 1 cm) No. 81 = Avignon-Digne, No. 84 = Marseille and Camargue, No. 93 = Rhône Valley and the Rhône Delta.

Marseille

Population: 878,000

The oldest of all the larger French cities, Marseille, is 2,500 years old and is the second largest city in France with a population approaching one million. Owing to the harbours, motorways, a good network of streets and the airport Marseille/Marignane, the city has an excellent infrastructure. The population is an international composite. This, however, does pose certain problems. This is especially true for the minority residents from the former North African colonies. A frightening development is the recent success of Le Pen's extremist right-wing political party "National Front."

Marseille / **History**

In 600 B.C., the Greeks arrived from Asia Minor to land on the coast of what is now Marseille. There, they encountered the original inhabitants, the Ligurians, who had settled here. According to a legend, their king organised a festival during which his daughter was to choose a husband, signalling this choice by presenting him with a chalice of wine. She chose the leader of the Greeks. After expanding the town of Massalia (so named by the Greeks) in cooperation with the Ligurians, the Greeks founded further trading posts in Arles, Nice and Antibes. They taught the inhabitants the techniques of wine production and olive cultivation. It was not long before the Ligurians felt threatened and fell into conflict with the Greeks. The city of Massalia also felt threatened and called upon the assistance of the Romans, who promptly heeded this call. During the course of the battles which followed, the Romans expanded their conquests in the Provence securing their territorial claims by founding new cities. The local inhabitants were driven further and further into the interior of the country. The populace and government of the city of Massalia were given a high degree of freedom in commerce. This was, however, to change during the 1st century A.D., when the city was drawn into the internal conflict between Caesar and Pompeius. Massalia sided with Pompeius, who was later defeated. When Caesar conquered Massalia after an occupation lasting six months, the city lost its significance and wealth. The city of Arles, founded by the Romans in 104 B.C., would assume this status. The situation was worsened by the attacks of foreign armies, which plundered Massalia. During the 13th century, however, this city (meanwhile called Marseille) experienced a renaissance. Resulting from the Crusades to Jerusalem, the harbour gained in significance, becoming an important port for ships departing for the Holy Land. At this time Marseille was an independent republic. As part of the Provence owned by Charles Anjou, Marseille fell under the rule of the French crown in 1481. The residents of Marseille, accustomed to independence, were not enthused with this development, as evidenced by the numerous uprising during the centuries to follow. An especially devastating year in the history of Marseille was 1720: the plague, brought over from Syria, claimed 50,000 lives — half of the city's population. The enthusiasm for the French Revolution (the anthem "La Marseillaise" is evidence of this) would rapidly fade, resulting from the Reign of Terror. This rejection brought the guillotine into the picture and many of Marseille's residents lost their lives. With the beginning of French participation in the colonial era, and the partial conquest of North Africa in the 19th century as well as the construction of the Suez Canal, Marseille and its harbour gained in significance. Today, this harbour is the second largest in Europe after Rotterdam.

Marseille / **Sights**

The search for Greek and Roman architecture in Marseille will prove futile with the exception of the ruins of a Greek city wall (3rd century B.C.) and portions of a Roman dock (1st century B.C.). There are two methods to explore the city: the first for those who arrive on Sunday because the city is loud and hectic during the week and would rather sit at the harbour and observed the bustle. The other method is for those who have a full day or several days to immerse themselves in the city. The view from the St-Nicolas Fort (17th century) of the city and the islands off the coast is a must for every visitor. Before beginning a sightseeing tour, one should stroll along the "La Canebière." The name is said to originate from the hemp fields (Chènevières), which were formerly located along the old harbour. The broad boulevard lined with shops, offices and cafés has a certain flair that one can hardly absorb. From there, one can quickly reach the old harbour, where the Greeks landed 2,500 years ago. Today, it is only used by sailboats, yachts and motor boats. Going along the Rue Paradis toward the sea one will reach the Notre-Dame-de-la-Gard on Rue Dragon. The massive building from the 19th century has a marble interior, which shimmers in various colours. The church tower with the large statue of Mary at its apex is the landmark of this city. The churches of Marseille include: first, the St-Victor Church, part of which originates from a monastery founded in the 5th century and destroyed during the French Revolution. The church is located across from the old harbour. After an Arab invasion in the 11th century, the church was rebuilt and expanded. During the 13th and 14th centuries, the impressive crypt was built and the exterior of the church took on the appearance of a fortress. During the 19th century, it was thoroughly renovated. Another church, also located near the old harbour, is the old Cathedral La Major (12th century). This Romanesque church was continually expanded. The three-naved church with its small tower has a noteworthy interior: exceptional appointments are the Lazarus Altar (15th century) and a reliquary from the 11th century. The new Cathedral La Major dates back to 1852 and is among the largest of its kind in France. Among the non-religious sights in Marseille are the following: the Hôtel de Ville (city hall) on the Quai du Porte, housed in a pompous Baroque building from the 17th century (be sure to take note of the entry hall). In addition are the former infirmaries in the Hospice de la Vieille Charité with its arcade walls over three stories high and a chapel from the 17th century. The Palais Longchamp at the end of Boulevard Longchamp, was built in the 19th century with arcades and fountains in the semi-circular centre portion. In its left wing is the Musée des Beaux-Arts with a wealth of sketches and French paintings from the 14th to 20th century and in its right wing, a museum of natural sciences. Marseille also has a wealth of museums including the Musée Cantini, located in the inner city and exhibiting a Fayence collection as well as the regional museum (Musée de Vieux Marseille) known for its significant Santons collection. Among the parks and gardens in Marseille, the Parc Borély with the castle (18th century) is recommended. The castle now houses the Musée d'Archéologie, displaying Greek and Roman archaeological finds. One will have a beautiful view from the Terrace in the Parc du Pharo near the St-Victor Church. Remaining to be mentioned is the new harbour from the mid 19th century; the wharfs can be toured on Sundays.

Marseille / **Practical Information**

Accommodation

Hotels: **** Sofitel Vieux Port, 36 boulevard Ch.-Livon, Tel: (91) 52 90 19, modern accommodation, restaurant with a view of the old harbour, 127 rooms 580-690 FF, complete meals 180-265 FF.

*** Résidence Bompard (without restaurant), 2 rue Flots-Bleus, Tel: (91) 52 10 93, 47 rooms 255-340 FF.

** Rome et St. Pierre (without restaurant), 7 cours St-Louis, Tel: (91) 54 19 52, 63 rooms 144-328 FF.

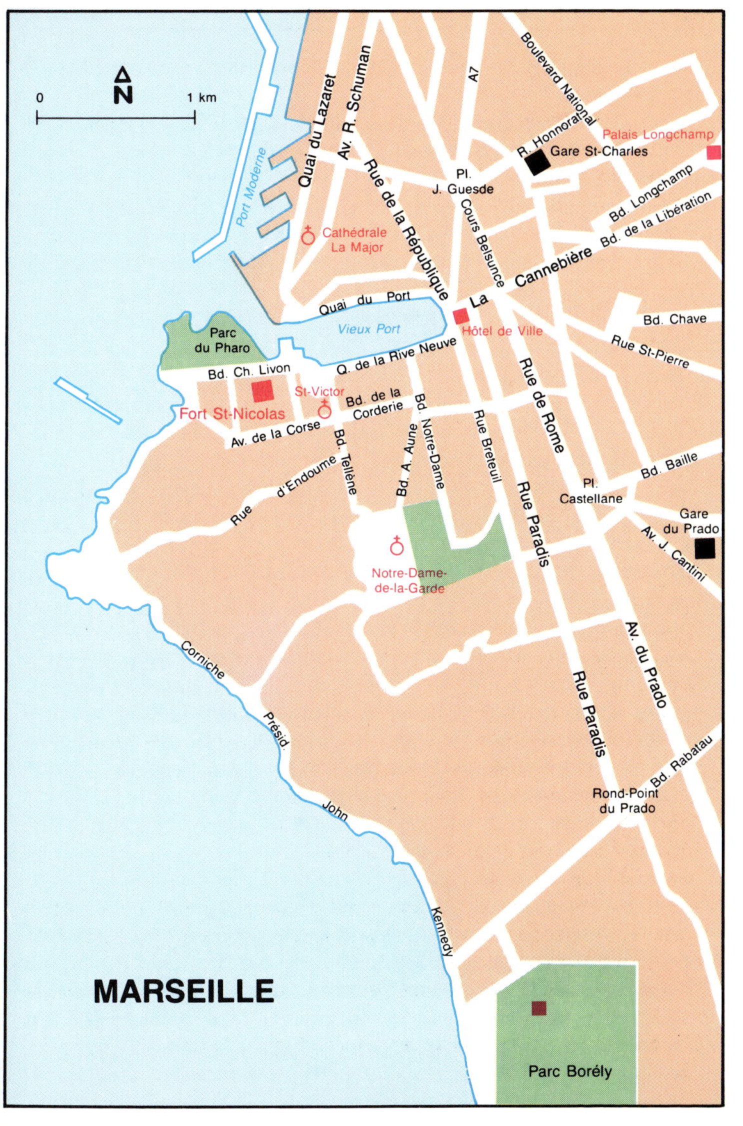
0
1 km
N
Port Moderne
Quai du Lazaret
Av. R. Schuman
Rue de la République
A7
Boulevard National
R. Honnorat
Gare St-Charles
Palais Longchamp
Pl.
J. Guesde
Cours Belsunce
Bd. Longchamp
Bd. de la Libération
Cathédrale
La Major
La Cannebière
Quai du Port
Vieux Port
Hôtel de Ville
Bd. Chave
Rue St-Pierre
Parc
du Pharo
Bd. Ch. Livon
Q. de la Rive Neuve
St-Victor
Bd. de la
Corderie
Fort St-Nicolas
Av. de la Corse
Bd. Tellène
Bd. A. Aune
Bd. Notre-Dame
Rue Breteuil
Rue de Rome
Rue d'Endoume
Pl.
Castellane
Bd. Baille
Gare
du Prado
Av. J. Cantini
Rue Paradis
Notre-Dame-
de-la-Garde
Corniche
Présid.
John
Kennedy
Av. du Prado
Rue Paradis
Bd. Rabatau
Rond-Point
du Prado
Parc Borély
MARSEILLE

* Martini, 5 Boulevard G.-Desplaces, Tel: (91) 64 11 17, 40 rooms 245-285 FF, complete meals 75-95 FF.
Youth Hostels: Château de Bois Luzy, avenue de Bois Luzy, Tel: (91) 49 06 18; Auberge de Marseille-Bonneveine, 47 avenue J. Vidal-Impasse Dr. Bonfils, Tel: (91) 73 21 81.
Beaches: The beaches are located to the south of the city and can be easily reached via the Corniche (Avenue J.F. Kennedy). An interesting alternative to these is located 38 km (24 miles) away on the Côte d'Azur, famous for its white wine and impressive coastal cliffs as well as the picturesque town of Cassis. From there one can reach Calanques to the east by driving down the D 559 (or even better by ship; docks at Quai St-Pierre), a coastal region punctuated with fjord-like coves.
Entertainment: Especially in summer, there are numerous festivals and folklore events. A detailed programme is available through the tourist information office as well as tickets for the concerts, choral performances, ballet etc. In addition, there are numerous discotheques, nightclubs, cinemas etc.
Medical Care: For on-call medical service, contact the police at Tel: (91) 91 90 40 and at night Tel: (91) 37 19 20; SOS-médecin, Tel: (91) 52 91 52.
Restaurants: *** Jambon de Parme, 67 rue La Palud, Tel: (91) 54 37 98, specialities à la carte 185-270 FF.
** Michel, 6 rue Catalans, Tel: (91) 52 30 63, fish specialities, 285-450 FF.
* La Charpenterie, 22 rue Paix, Tel: (91) 54 22 89, complete meals 90-140 FF.
Shopping: There is a daily fish market from 7 to 9 am at quai des Belges. In a city of this size, there is, of course, a huge selection of shops. One point that should be mentioned has to do with the peddlers, Arab brocanteurs, who sell jewellry, leather goods and antiques. They can get quite insistent, but one should not let oneself be talked into buying something.
Sports Facilities: An 18-hole golf course is located about 22 km (14 miles) north of the city, Tel: (42) 24 20 41.
Transportation: Marseille is an important transportation hub. The international airport (the second largest in France, approximately 28 km (17½ miles) north of the city) has flights to over 50 cities in the world. There are also ship routes to the significant Mediterranean harbours: car ferries, for example, to Corsica (61 Boulevard des Dames, Tel: (91) 56 32 00). There are also numerous direct train connections to the centrally located train station (for trains transporting cars contact Tel: (91) 08 50 50). Marseille is also readily accessible by motorway: via A7 from Paris/Lyon, via A8 from Aix-en-Provence, via A9 from

Spain/Languedoc. Within the city, however, one should use the public transportation with its numerous bus and subway routes.
Important Addresses: Office de Tourisme, 4 Canebière, Tel: (91) 54 91 11.

Maubec

From Cavaillon on the D 2, heading toward Coustellet/Gordes, one must turn onto the D 29 or D 144 after about 7 km (4½ miles).
Camping: ** Camping les Royères du Prieuré Municipal La Combe St-Pierre (100 sites), Tel: (90) 76 50 34.
Horseback Riding and Rental: André Pavon, Le Clos de Princes, Tel: (90) 71 90 29 and (90) 71 70 91 for television, films, weddings, parades etc.

Medical Care

In every larger city there are pharmacies and physicians. In an emergency, contact the Gendarmerie or Police. They will be of assistance or will call an ambulance on one's behalf. Before beginning one's holiday travels one should contact one's health insurance agent to confirm the details of coverage in a foreign country. Treatment expenses must usually be paid immediately and are then later reimbursed upon returning home. Those who would like comprehensive health coverage during their holidays can purchase a travel health insurance policy.

Medication

In addition to personal medication, it is recommended to bring along suntan lotion with a sufficiently high protection factor. Also, in case one underestimates the intensity of the sun in the Provence, an ointment for sunburn is recommended. One should also be careful of the insects in the Provence: the French spray their fields heavily with insecticides. The consequence of this is that the insects' blood has a relatively high concentration of insecticides. An insect bite can cause infections and swelling — and this, not only for those sensitive to insect bites. If medication does not ease the pain and/or swelling, one should visit a doctor.

Ménerbes

Population: about 1,000; elevation: 224 metres (733 feet)
On the D 3/D 109 between Oppède-le-Vieux and Bonnieux is Ménerbes, a historically interesting town named after the Roman goddess Minerva and situated on the slopes of Luberon.

Ménerbes / **History**

The history of this small town is closely connected to the Waldensians (Vaudois). Here, in a secluded but accessible mountainous location, this area was a sanctuary for the last members of the Waldensian sect for five years in the 16th century. This lasted until they succumb to the dominating power of the Catholic Church. The survivors fled to higher-lying areas or escaped to the bordering countries. Today, the ruins of the castle still tower above the town, reminiscent of a turbulent and violent past.

Ménerbes / **Sights**

From the parking area near the Clémentine Restaurant, one has a wonderful view of the Vaucluse plain. The fortified castle in Ménerbes is, unfortunately, not open to the public. This served as a sanctuary for the Waldensians. The St-Antonin Chapel dates back to the 12th century.

Ménerbes / **Practical Information**

Accommodation: ** Host. Le Roy Soleil, 2 km (1¼ miles) via the D 3, Tel: (90) 72 25 61, modern accommodation, 14 rooms 320-620 FF, complete meals 160-250 FF.
Restaurants: Clémentine, Tel: (90) 72 32 81.

Mérindol

Population: about 1,000
Mérindol is approximately 18 km (11¼ miles) southeast of Cavaillon on the D 973. Mérindol counts as an especially historical and especially tragic site for the French Protestants. In the development of the bloody prosecution of the Waldensians *(→History)*, this town, considered a centre for the religious group, was completely destroyed.

Money

The currency of France is the French Franc (1 FF = 100 Centimes). The constantly changing exchange rate was 100 FF = £ 10.10 (100 FF = $ 18.42) in May 1992. At present the downward trend in the value of the French Franc continues. Almost all of the banks and some post offices will accept Eurocheques (maximum per check = 1,400 FF). In addition, one can withdraw money

Another side to the Provence: the colourful activity of the harbour cities on the shores of the Mediterranean ▶

BAR LE PORT
RESTAURANT LA VOUTE
CASSIS
CASSIS

in France from one's postal savings account (a maximum of about £ 330/ $ 588 per day and up to £ 660/$ 1176 within 30 days). The French accept credit cards readily. When shopping, it is more common to pay by credit card than with cash.

Montmajour (Monastery)

Montmajour / **History**

Montmajour is situated northwest of Arles and is accessible via the D 17. It was a former monastery which was surrounded by swamp land up until the 10th century. Originally, there was only a Christian cemetery, maintained by the residents of the area. Later, Benedictine monks founded a monastery on this site. Because of the inherent building conditions, the swamp had to be drained and dried and the ground prepared for construction. The so-called Pardon of Montmajour (a sale of indulgences) was decisive in the decision to further develop and expand the monastery in the 11th century. This source of church revenues, prevalent during all of the Middle Ages, made rapid and extensive expansion of the monastery possible. The monastery soon enjoyed widespread repute as a place of pilgrimage. Its decline began in the 17th century, when mores became more lax, making it necessary for the Archbishop of Arles to intervene. The Benedictines resisted and soon a conflict developed with the military. The monks were ultimately driven out by the military which had the support of the Archbishop. A short time later, there was a minor renaissance and the damaged portions of the buildings were restored. However, due to the involvement of the abbot in the collier affair centred around Marie Antoinette, the monastery was closed in 1786. The building and its contents were auctioned off and only the purchase of this monastery in 1838 by the city of Arles saved it from complete decay.

Montmajour / **Sights**

Many of the sights consist only of ruins. Among the building which are still intact is the church from the 12th century, impressive because of its unadorned architecture and the massive crypt, partially embedded in the cliffs. The cloister is quite noteworthy: with its columns decorated with plastics, it counts among the most beautiful in the Provence. The motifs used depict scenes from antiquity to the Middle Ages. From the Donjon (14th century; the Abbot's Tower) one has a fantastic panorama far across the Crau plain. A little further one will reach the original chapel, Chapelle St-Pierre, built in the 11th century and partially carved from the cliffs.

Motorway Tolls

The French motorway network is very good. Relatively expensive tolls are raised for the use of the motorways. When entering the motorway, one automatically passes a toll booth where a ticket is dispensed when the button is pressed. When exiting the motorway, one pays for the distance travelled. Sometimes, there are machines at the motorway exits. This makes it advisable to have some change in French currency ready. Other times there are toll booths where one can pay in notes. Since recently, motorway tolls can be paid by credit card.

Murs

Population: 300; elevation: 530 metres (1,733 feet)
Murs is situated somewhat remotely on the D 4 about 18 kilometres (11¼ miles) from Apt. Still it is not all that difficult to find. This is the location of the house where Crillon the Brave (1543-1615) stood in battle with King Henry IV. The Romanesque façade was constructed in the 13th century. Also worth seeing is the restored Renaissance castle from the 15th and 16th century (now privately owned and unfortunately not open to the public). During the epidemic of the plague in 1720, an 11 mile long "plague wall" was constructed. Today only a few remnants in the area around Murs can still be seen.
Hotel: Le Crillon, Tel: (90) 72 02;
Camping: ** Camping municipal des Charlottes (120 sites), Tel: (90) 72 05 38.

Nesque Canyon

The Gorges de la Nesque is the bed of the Nesque River, cut deep into the rock. One can experience the beauty of this canyon on a drive along the winding D 924 from Mazan to Sault. From Villes-sur-Auzon, the drive begins to get interesting because this marks the beginning of the canyon. At this point it is still hidden under shrubs and trees but during the next 11 kilometres (7 miles) to Monieux it can be seen quite well. There is a breathtaking view from the observation point Belvedère.

Nîmes

Population: 130,000; elevation: 39 metres (128 feet)
Nîmes is accessible from Orange or Avignon via the A 9. It is situated on the border with the Département of Gard. The present day city is lively and

somewhat loud, a result of the industrial works. It is full of old buildings and is definitely worth visiting. Nîmes is, furthermore the birthplace of Alphonse Daudet *(→Fontvielle).*

Nîmes / **History**

After being founded by the Gauls, Nîmes became a Roman veteran colony under the rule of Augustus. A city wall was erected relatively early in its history as were a number of impressive structures, including an amphitheatre. The importance of Nîmes to the Romans is made apparent through the construction of an aqueduct *(→Pont du Gard),* because the water supply for the rapidly growing city in the 2nd century (some set the population at 50,000, others at 200,000) threatened collapse. Nîmes lost this status during the migration of nations and the decline of the Roman Empire. Arabs and Goths invaded the city well into the early Middle Ages, and this was amplified by the religious wars. Thus, Nîmes sided with the Albigensians during the 12th century when it was the territory of the Count of Toulouse. The subsequent self-declared Crusade by the pope and the king of France nipped the uprising in the bud and Nîmes was incorporated into the French kingdom. However, during the 16th century, the city of Nîmes sympathised with the Calvinists and they once again became the brunt of a penal expedition by the king. This series of religious conflicts was only to come to an end with the French Revolution. Nîmes could find the peace to expand economically. It became a centre for the production of wine and manufacturing light cotton fabrics, which (when imported from India) were called "Indiennes." Nîmes has maintained this significance up to the present.

Nîmes / **Sights**

The points of interest in Nîmes are best explored on foot. There is also a combined ticket available for all of the significant sights of the city. The ring of boulevards connecting and surrounding all of the principal sights also makes a sightseeing tour quite convenient. On the Place des Arènes (parking areas are also located here) stands the best preserved Roman theatre. The exterior façade is comprised of 60 levels punctuated by rounded arches. The oval shaped amphitheatre, built in the first century A.D. has the outer dimensions of 134 metres (438 feet) in length with a width of 103 metres (337 feet). Its height is 22 metres (72 feet), while the arena itself has a length of 69 metres (226 feet) and a width of 38 metres (125 feet). The terrace-like spectator area could accommodate 22,000 people, who could enter the arena through one of the

124 entrances. After an interlude by the Goths, who expanded the arena as a fortress in the 5th century, the poorest of the poor settled with their ramshackle huts in the interior of the arena during the Middle Ages. It was only in the 19th century that the arena regained its old appearance through extensive renovations. At the end of the Boulevard Victor-Hugo, when looking from the arena, is the Maison Carrée, located on Rue Général-Perrier. This is another Roman construction measuring 27 metres (88 feet) in length, 14 metres (46 feet) in width and reaching a height of 17 metres (56 feet). This temple was built by Augustus for his family. During the course of history, this building housed every thing from the city hall to horse stalls. Across from this, on Rue Auguste is the tourist information office, formerly the location of the Forum Romanum. To the west of this is the Jardin (garden) de la Fontaine, which can be reached by walking down Quai de la Fontaine. This beautiful park laid out with terraces, fountains and statues dates back to the period from 1744 to 1755. Within the park are the ruins of the Temple of Diana, built on the site of the springs, a Roman sanctum. Another point of interest in the park is the Tour Magne (1st century B.C.), a 30 metre (98 foot) high tower which is all that is left of the former fortress. Going back over the Quai de la Fontaine into the old city, one will pass by several patrician house from the Renaissance. The former, original Romanesque Notre-Dame-et-St-Castor was rebuilt during the 19th century. Not far from here, one will come upon the Musée du Vieux Nîmes, a regional museum housed in a palais from the 17th century. The Musée des Beaux-Arts, located somewhat outside of the old city has, among other things, a large, well preserved mosaic and a collection of paintings from the 16th to 20th centuries. The house where Alphonse Daudet was born is on Boulevard Gambetta, house number 22. Nearby is the Porte d'Arles, through which the Via Domitia led to the forum in 15 B.C.

Nîmes / **Practical Information**

Accommodation

Hotels: **** Imperator Concorde, place A. Briand, Tel: (66) 21 90 30, 65 rooms 335-650 FF, complete meals 150-280 FF.

*** Louvre, 2 square Couronne, Tel: (66) 67 22 75, 28 rooms 250-350 FF, complete meals 82-180 FF.

** Carrière, 6 rue Grizot, Tel: (66) 67 24 89, 55 rooms 200-250 FF, complete meals 60-115 FF.

** Amphithéâtre (without restaurant), 4 rue Arènes, Tel: (66) 67 28 51, 21 rooms 100-190 FF.

Camping: Camping Domaine de la Bastide, Tel: (66) 38 09 21.
Youth Hostels: Chemin de la Cigale, Tel: (66) 23 25 04.
Automobile Repair: Alfa-Romeo-SEAT, Austin-Rover, BMW, Citroën, Fiat, Ford, Mercedes-Benz, Peugeot-Talbot, Renault, Toyota, VW, Volvo.
Entertainment: Information on various special events (festivals, concerts etc.) in this city is available through the tourist information office. In addition, there are eight discotheques, just as many cinemas and six theatres.
Medical Care: On-call emergency medical assistance Tel: (66) 67 00 00; Hospital, 5 rue Hoche, Tel: (66) 27 41 11.
Restaurants: ** Le Magister, 5 rue National, Tel: (66) 76 11 00, complete meals 165-195 FF.
** Restaurant Le Lisita, 2 Arènes, Tel: (66) 67 29 15, complete meals 100-140 FF.
About 9 km (5½ miles) south toward the airport in Garons: *** Alexandre, Tel: (66) 70 08 99, (highly recommended specialities) complete meals 205-260 FF.
Shopping: Mondays: boulevard Jean-Jaurès, flower and flea market, boulevard Gambetta general market; Tuesdays: avenue Bir Hakeim and Fridays, boulevard Jean-Jaurès fresh produce market; Sundays: flea market surrounding the St-Baudile Church.
Sports Facilities: About 11 km (7 miles) south of the city is an 18-hole golf course, Tel: (66) 70 17 37; four swimming pools, tennis courts, horseback riding.
Transportation: Bus terminal: Tel: (66) 29 52 00.
Train station: 1 boulevard Talabot, Tel: (66) 23 50 50.
Approximately 8 km (5 miles) south of town is the airport Nîmes-Garons, Tel: (66) 70 06 88 (four flights to Paris daily).
Important Addresses: Office de Tourisme, 6 rue Auguste, Tel: (66) 67 29 11 and place Arènes, Tel: (66) 21 02 51.
Post Office: boulevard Gambetta, Tel: (66) 67 29 02.

Notre-Dame de Lumières

Halfway between Cavaillon and Apt on the N 100 is one of the famous sites of pilgrimage in the Provence, Notre-Dame de Lumières. The church gained fame in the 17th century through mysterious luminescent phenomena and the miraculous healing of an old farmer. To accommodate the steadily increasing influx of pilgrims, a larger church was built over the old Romanesque chapel at the end of the 17th century. Hanging at the side aisles of this church are a number of interesting →*votive pictures.* In the original chapel which now serves as a crypt, the sky-blue, luminescent "Our Beloved Lady of the Lights" may appear tacky at first glance but will then enthral the observer.

Oppède-le-Vieux

Population: around 1,000; elevation: 180-300 metres (589-981 feet)

Oppède-le-Vieux is situated east of Cavaillon (turn off the N 100 onto the D 178). One should not be confused: behind the new village of Oppède, Les Poulivets, the road continues toward Luberon to old Oppède. One will also see it from quite a distance along the chilly northern slopes where the sun can only warm the town during the height of summer. The town was uninhabited since the beginning of this century and fell into decay until, in recent years, it was discovered by a number of artists (although none of them starving). These artists settled here and, working painstakingly with an eye for detail and a healthy portion of idealism, they restored the buildings not only beautifully but historically exact. This town is rich in history: Jean Meynier d'Oppède ruled from the castle above the town, and prosecuted the Waldensians under the auspices of Francis I. From the new parking area at the base of the town, one can climb up through the steep old alleyways (appropriate shoes are necessary) up to the fortress. Along the way one will be taken back to the Middle Ages. Upon arriving at the fortress one will see the Romanesque Notre-Dame d'Alydon from the 11th to 13th century (restored from the 14th to 16th century) and the ruins of the fortress complex. The fortress is in an advanced state of decay making it dangerous to climb about within the crumbling and unsecured walls. The location of the fortress gives an impression of how difficult it must have been to conquer: surrounded by steep cliffs and the rugged caves of the Luberon. From this vantage point, one has a wonderful view of the Vaucluse plain.

Orange

Population: approximately 27,000; elevation: 46 metres (150 feet)

Orange, 31 km (19½ miles) north of Avignon is considered the gateway to the Provence.

Orange / **History**

As is the case with most of the cities in the Provence, Orange was founded before the arrival of the Romans. The Celts settled in the on the hill of Saint-Eutrope and founded the city, which served as the backdrop for a large battle in 105 B.C. This was between the Kimbers and Teutons united in battle against the Romans. The Romans were decisively defeated, and could first found a representative settlement there in the year 36 B.C. Orange rapidly developed into an important city; the buildings which have endured over the years are proof of a splendid past. With the mass exodus in 412 A.D., this city was destroyed by the Visigoths. In the 16th century, Orange fell under the ownership of the House of Nassau; Prince William of Nassau, the governor of the Netherlands, changed his name from this point on to William of Orange. Under the Nassau-Orange rule, the city of Orange flourished; a wall was soon erected around the city and a castle built. With the end of the war between France and Holland (1672-1678), Orange fell under French rule and Louis XIV had the fortification walls razed. Today, Orange is part of the Département of Vaucluse and is home to the vegetable, fruit and canning industries.

Orange / **Sights**

The significant buildings in Orange are all quite close to each other, making it easy to reach them all on foot. When coming into the city from the north on the N 7, visitors will pass the l'arc de Triomphe, somewhat outside the city. It has three arcades and originates from the years 21 to 26 A.D. It measures 20 metres (65 feet) in width and has a height of 18 metres (59 feet). The relief embellishments depict the battles and victories of the Gauls. During the Middle Ages, the gate was a part of the city wall and was restored to its original condition during the 19th century. To the south on the Place de Frères Mounet is the extremely well preserved Roman theatre was built under Augustus in the first century B.C. The impressive façade measures 103 metres (337 feet) in length and is 37 metres (121 feet) high. The theatre could accommodate around 11,000 visitors. Unfortunately, the marble veneer of the back stage wall is no longer completely intact. In this theatre is the 3.55 metre (12 foot) tall statue of Caesar Augustus. On the west side of the theatre, excavations uncovered remnants from the former sports complex which once measured 400 x 80 metres (1,308 x 262 feet). In addition, the ruins of a temple complex were found. Behind the sports complex, when heading out of the city, is the Colline St-Eutrope, the municipal hill. Today, this serves as a public park. Passing the remains of a fortress, one will have a panoramic view of the city and its environs. The walk down the hill leads past the theatre and the Musée Municipal, which exhibits a Roman land registry map engraved in marble as well as other archaeological finds. From here, one can take a stroll through the old city by the beautiful houses to the Notre-Dame Cathedral. The façade originates from the 12th century and suffered greatly as a result of the religious wars. Portions of the interior of the cathedral date back to the Romanesque Period.

Orange / **Practical Information**

Accommodation

Hotels: *** Altéa Euromotel, route de Caderousse, Tel: (90) 34 24 10, modern accommodation, 99 rooms 295-340 FF, complete meals 90-135 FF.

** Louvre et Terminus, 89 avenue F.-Mistral, Tel: (90) 34 10 08, 34 rooms 190-280 FF, complete meals 70-120 FF.

** H. Arène (without restaurant), place de Langes, Tel: (90) 34 10 95, 30 rooms 210-280 FF.

** Glacier (without restaurant), 46 cours A.-Briand, Tel: (90) 34 02 01, 28 rooms 180-200 FF.

* Ibis, route Caderousse at the eastern end of town, Tel: (90) 34 35 35, 66 rooms 250-270 FF, complete meals 80-120 FF.

Camping: ** Le Jonquier, rue Alexis Carrel, Tel: (90) 34 19 83, tennis, miniature golf, archery.

An attraction for a number of photographers: the unique light effects in the Provence

Automobile Repair: Alfa-Romeo, BMW, Citroën, Fiat, Lancia-Autobianchi, Ford, Opel-GM, Peugeot-Talbot, Renault, Toyota, VW.
Car Rental: Europcar, 68 cours A. Briand, Tel: (90) 51 67 53; Hertz, 11-13 boulevard Edouard Daladier, Tel: (90) 34 00 34.
Entertainment: From the middle of July to the beginning of August, large outdoor performances take place in the classical theatre. The programme for the operas, concerts and tickets are available through the tourist information office. Be sure to order tickets early enough.
Medical Care: On-call medical assistance through the police station, Tel: (90) 51 71 04; medical centre, rue de Bretagne, Tel: (90) 34 57 02.
Restaurants: ** Le Pigriallet, chemin colline St-Eutrope, Tel: (90) 34 44 25, good specialities, complete meals 130-210 FF.
** Le Forum, 3 rue du Mazeau, Tel: (90) 34 01 09, complete meals 85-140 FF.
Shopping: The market takes place on Thursdays.
Sports Facilities: In Orange, there are three swimming pools, fishing: on the Rhône; horseback riding: Club équestre du 1er R.E.C. route du d'Artillerie, Tel: (90) 51 63 85.
Transportation: Orange is on the train route through the Rhône Valley with connections to Avignon, Arles, Marseille, Cavaillon etc.; train station: Avenue Frédéric Mistral, Tel: (90) 34 17 82.
Important Addresses: Office de Tourisme and Accueil de France: Course Aristide-Briand, Tel: (90) 34 70 88 and (90) 34 22 85.
Town Hall: place G. Clémenceau, Tel: (90) 51 80 06.
Post Office: Avenue Edouard Daladier, Tel: (90) 34 08 70.

Pernes-les-Fontaines

Population: 700; elevation: 100 metres (327 feet)
The picturesque water city of Pernes-les-Fontaines lies about 8 kilometres (5 miles) from Carpentras on the D 938. Bisected by the Nesque River, over 30 fountains are spread out over the town, leading to its epithet. Earlier, Pernes was the capital of Comtat Venaissin. Today, Pernes lives from the cultivation of fruit and vegetables, as do so many towns in the Provence.

Pernes-les-Fontaines / **Sights**

Pernes-les-Fontaines is best explored on foot. Through narrow alleyways, one can stroll by old buildings, tranquil corners, dozing cats, flower beds and fountains. On the banks of the Nesque River (which were, unfortunately, artificially straightened) in the centre of town a small area consisting of the Notre Dame

Gate (Porte-Notre-Dame) from the 16th century as well as a small bridge, a chapel and a tower. These were formerly owned by the Count of Toulouse. Directly in front of the gate is the most interesting fountain, the Cormoran fountain, from the 18th century. The other fountains located throughout the city are also worth seeing. On the northern banks of the river is the Notre-Dame-de-Nazareth. Its oldest portions date back to the 11th century. Not far from here on a small square located among the houses, one will see the most famous sight: the square Ferrande Tower from the 13th century. In the third story of this tower are frescoes which also date back to the same period. Tours are offered daily; information on exact times is available from the tourist information office (during the low season these are only on Saturdays and Sundays from 10 am to noon). Other buildings worth seeing include: the town hall, housed in a palace from the 17th century with a beautiful fountain in the atrium; the Porte de Villeneuve; and the remains of Porte de St-Gilles from the 16th century, once part of the city's fortifications.

Pernes-les-Fontaines / **Practical Information**

Accommodation: ** Prato Plage-L'Hermitage (without restaurant), route Carpentras, Tel: (90) 66 51 41, 20 rooms 200-280 FF.

Shopping: Market on Sundays; wine: Cave Coopérative "La Pernoise," Michel Aguillon "Les Eysserides."

Important Addresses: Tourist Information: Pont de la Nesque, Tel: (90) 61 31 04.

Pertuis

Population: 12,430; elevation: 210 metres (688 feet)

Le Pertuis means passageway or narrows. The town is located about 35 kilometres southeast of Apt on the D 973, the southern gateway to Luberon. It is a small, lively city on the banks of the Lèze River.

Pertuis / **Sights**

In the centre of this town is the St-Nicolas Church built in 1600, in addition to the ruins of a medieval château. The interior of the church is furnished with a winged altar piece and other treasures from this time period. Two towers from the 13th and 14th centuries add to the town's profile.

Pertuis / **Practical Information**

Accommodation

Hotels: *** Sevan, modern accommodation, route manosque, 1.5 km (1 mile) from town, Tel: (90) 79 19 30, 32 rooms 344-442 FF, complete meals 110-240 FF.
** Le Quatre Septembre, 60 place du 4 septembre, Tel: (90) 79 01 52, 15 rooms.
Camping: *** Camping municipal Les Pinèdes, at the eastern end of town, Avenue Pierre Augier, (800 sites), Tel: (90) 79 10 98.

Automobile Repair: Fiat, Ford, Renault.

Medical Care: Hospital, Tel: (90) 79 13 33, there are also a number of physicians and pharmacies in Pertuis.

Restaurants: ** L'Aubarestiëro, place Garcin, Tel: (90) 79 14 74, with 13 rooms 130-240 FF, complete meals 80-320 FF.
* Le Quatre Septembre, 60 place du 4 septembre, Tel: (90) 79 01 52, complete meals 55-115 FF.
* L'Escapade, route Manosque, 1.5 km (1 mile) from town, Tel: (90) 79 03 09, complete meals 65-75 FF.

Shopping: Market on Fridays; Cave Coopérative.

Transportation: Train station S.N.C.F., Tel: (90) 79 10 43
Bus routes to Avignon, Marseille, Aix-en-Provence, Banon etc.

Important Addresses: Office de Tourisme: Le Donjon, place Mirabeau, Tel: (90) 79 15 56.
Town Hall: Tel: (90) 79 02 74.
Gendarmerie/Police: Tel: (90) 79 10 38.
Post Office: Parc Granier, Tel: (90) 79 10 78.

Pharmacies

There are pharmacies in all larger cities. These can be recognised by a green cross on their sign. Business hours are not the same all over France, but will be the same as the local business hours. The nearest pharmacy which is open Sundays and holidays will also be displayed.

Some important terms:

physician	médecin
diarrhoea	diarrhée
cold	refroidissement
fever	fièvre
sore throat	mal de gorge

A peaceful village square far away from the hurry of the everyday ▶

adhesive bandage	emplâtre
cough	toux
insect bite	piqûre d'insecte
charcoal tablets	charbon
headache	mal de tête
ointment	onguent
pains	doulers
sunburn	coup de soleil
tablet	comprimé
drops	gouttes
constipation	constipation
dentist	chirugien dentiste
toothache	mal de dents
suppository	suppositoire

Photography

One should bring along ample film since this is relatively expensive in France. There is certainly plenty to photograph in the Provence, but one should choose carefully: mental impressions of the sleepy little villages and their residents will most likely outlast those seen through a camera lens.

Pont du Gard

Northeast of Nîmes on the D 981 is the Roman aqueduct Pont du Gard. This aqueduct is a highlight of Roman architecture, built in the year 19 B.C. to ensure the water supply for the nearby city of Nîmes. Originally, the aqueduct was 50 km (31 miles) long and transported a quantity of almost 20,000 cubic metres (706,312 cubic feet) of water daily from a spring located near Uzès to Nîmes. The blocks weighing up to 6 tons each were stacked without using mortar. The remaining portions are still impressive with a lower length of 142 metres (465 feet), an upper length of 275 metres (900 feet) and a height of 49 metres (160 feet), giving an impression of Roman achievements in the area of architecture.
Vers/Pont du Gard: Camping de Valive, Tel: (66) 22 81 52.
Camping International Gorges du Gardon, Tel: (66) 22 81 81.

Population

Including the Côte d'Azur, the region encompasses an area of about 15,000 square kilometres (5,850 square miles), in which about 3.5 million people live.

The majority live in the metropolitan areas of Marseille, Nîmes, Aix-en-Provence, Avignon, Arles and Orange as well as along the coast. If considering the subdivision by Départements, then Vaucluse (3,500 square kilometres/1,365 square miles; with a population of 400,000) also has a high population density in its metropolitan areas of Avignon, Apt and Carpentras. The rural regions, in contrast, have a very low population density.

Postal Service

In addition to at post offices, postage stamps can also be purchased in tobacco shops (Bureaux de Tabac). One can also buy stamps from machines; these books of stamps (Carnet) have ten stamps worth 2.20 FF each. Postage for a postcard is 2 FF; for a letter up to 20 grams, 2.20 FF.

letter	lettre
postage stamps	timbres-poste
to Great Britain/the United States	à Grande Britaigne/États-Uni

Provençal Language

As is the case with all of the romantic languages, French developed from Latin, which was spoken in the regions under Roman rule. The language developed in two directions: depending whether the word "yes" was pronounced as "oc" or "oil" (which later became "oui"), French was subdivided in Langue d'oc and Langue d'oil. Occitaine, the linguistic region of Old Provençal formerly encompassed all of southern France and into the northern regions, with a linguistic border extending from Lyon to Bordeaux. Resulting from the Troubadour's poetry, this language flourished and became known beyond the borders in Italy, Germany and England. In the 16th century, the northern French language was declared the official language. Provençale was still widely spoken among a large proportion of the population, and was maintained in literature and folklore. It was only in the 19th century that a group of poets, the "Félibrige," once again revived the Provençale language. Novels, poems and songs were written, but the colloquial language; however, the occitaine language did not establish itself as was hoped. The most widely known among these poets, Frédéric Mistral, completely dedicated himself to this literary direction. He received the Nobel prize for his work 'Mirèio' — 'Mireille' in 1904. With this money, he financed the folk museum Museon Arlatan in →*Arles.* In addition, he published a dictionary of the Provençal language, which is used today as the basis for the study of the Occitaine linguistics. Characteristics of Provençal speech are long ou's, aa's, shrill sounding li's and the peculiarity of pronouncing silent endings. Most words do not appear to be French. Often, one can read the word 'lou' on restaurant signs or menus — this is the equivalent of the French article le or les. The word 'oc' on the walls of some buildings or houses is the slogan of a political movement, fighting for the reestablishment of Occitaine, the original linguistic area with 31 Départements.

Puyvert

Population: 230; elevation: 250 metres (818 feet)
When approaching from Cavaillon on the D 973, one must turn onto the D 27 near Lauris heading toward Lourmarin.
The Waldensian village of Puyvert was completely destroyed in 1545. The village was repopulated in 1618.

Religion

After Constantine proclaimed the Tolerance Edict in Milan in 313, including the acceptance of Christianity, the growth of Christianity began in the Provence. At the end of the 11th century, the concept of the Crusades appeared. Pope Urban II called for the first crusades from French territory. The idea met with Louis XI's enthusiasm and he set off from Aigues-Mortes (which had been expanded in 1248 for just that reason) for the 6th and 7th Crusades in 1270. During the seventh Crusade, Louis fell victim to the plague upon landing in Tunis. However, during the 20 years before his death the fierce Albingensian Crusade (1209-1229) cost tens of thousands of Frenchmen their lives. A reform began in the 12th century originating from Albi, named the Albigensian movement, considered the present world evil. Since they rejected a great deal of church dogma, they fell into conflict with Pope Innocent III. Supported by cities such as Les Baux and personalities like the ruler of the Provence, Count Toulouse, the sect's popularity spread rapidly. Louis XI was interested in the count's land and together with the pope, he called for a crusade against the heathens. At the end of the holy war, the King of France gained not only the land but influence over the Provence. The church was given the land around Avignon, the Comtat Venaissin. In the 16th century, a second religious war shook the Provence, once again incited by the persecution of a religious sect. This time the object of prosecution was the Waldensian sect, named after its founder Peter Waldo (12th century) from Lyon. The Waldensians lived according to the strict moral teachings of Calvin and in poverty. They lived predominantly in the Provence (Luberon) and were a constant thorn in the side of the Catholic Church. This was sufficient for Francis I to entrust the prosecution of the Waldensians to the President of Aix-en-Provence, Jean Meynier d'Oppède in 1545. His avarice for land prompted him to incite a virtual bloodbath among the Waldensians. Numerous towns in the Luberon region like Ménerbes, Mérindol or Puyvert were levelled and their residents were either killed or sentenced to galley slavery. The eradication of the Waldensians sect was only the beginning of Protestant prosecution (Huguenots), which lasted from 1560-1598. This clash between the Catholic establishment and the Calvinist Huguenots was carried out with bitterness and brutality. In the city of Nîmes, for example, the Catholics slaughtered hundreds of Huguenots in their delusions of religious exclusivity. These battles were ended by Henry IV with his conversion to the Catholic faith and the subsequent edict of Nantes (1598). However, roughly one hundred years later, Louis XIV revoked the edict and the prosecution of the Protestants began anew. Cardinal Richelieu ordered the destruction of cities and fortress sympathising with the Protestants *(→Les Baux).* Those who survived, fled to other countries. Through these actions, the Catholic Church in collaboration with the French crown had finally quashed

A meeting point for a pastis or rosé: a quaint sidewalk café nestled in the shade

the Protestant movement. Today, there are 45.5 million Catholics in comparison to 800,000 Protestants in France.

Restaurants

Even though France is famous all over the world for its cuisine, this is not a guarantee that one can eat well everywhere in France. There is good reason that the famous "Michelin Guide" is so successful. A change in chefs or management has often forced top restaurants to close overnight. Restaurants included in this guide are merely listed; The case with hotels, the restaurants in France are subdivided into categories based mainly on price.

Roquefavour (Aqueduct)

Twelve kilometres (7½ miles) west of Aix-en-Provence on the D 64, one will come upon this "replica" of the Pont-du-Gard. The Marseille canal crosses the Arc Valley at this point. The aqueduct was built from 1842 to 1847. The canal bridge has three stories, is 375 metres (1,226 feet) long and 83 metres (272 feet) high.
Hotel: ** Arquier, Tel: (42) 24 20 45, 18 rooms 80-220 FF, meals 90-230 FF.

Roussillon

Population: about 1,300; elevation: 390 metres (1,275 feet)
Roussillon is located ten kilometres west of Apt. This is the famous red ochre town, which is heavily visited during the summer months. The houses shimmer in different tones of red and yellow depending on the time of day.

Roussillon / **Sights**

It is best to park one's car at the parking area near the post office. From there, a path to the left leads uphill to an observation point, offering a view of the town and surrounding countryside. A little further to the right, one will pass by a cemetery and come upon a small footpath leading to the "Chaussée des Géants" (Giants' Street) which in turn leads to the ochre cliffs, shimmering in all shades of colour. Another beautiful view is from the Castrum, near the Romanesque church built in the 12th century, which is at the highest point in the village. Roussillon has also gained literary fame: the American Sociologist Laurence Willie observed the typical lifestyle of a Provençal village here. He lived here for several years with his family in Roussillon in order to participate in the daily routine and to gain more precise insight. The result of his study, "Village in Vaucluse," was a best seller. Although it is described as a village like many others, this book is enthralling because many of the customs and habits are described in detail. The second literary figure connected with this town is Samuel Beckett. Beckett hid here during the German occupation and wrote his novel "Watt" (and not "Waiting for Godot" as is often incorrectly stated).

Roussillon / **Practical Information**

Accommodation

Hotels: *** Mas de Garrigon, 2 km (1¼ miles) via the D 2 and C 7, Tel: (90) 05 63 22, attractive with a view of the Luberon, modern accommodation, 8 rooms 565-600 FF, complete meals from 200 FF.

** Résidence des Ocres (without restaurant), route Gordes, Tel: (90) 05 60 50, 16 rooms 240-280 FF.

Hotel-Pension-Restaurant Chez Georgette, place de la Marie, Tel: (90) 75 61 07.

Chambres d'hôtes : Poterie de Pierroux, Claire et Jean-Philippe Fruchart, on the D 199 toward Apt, Tel: (90) 05 68 81.

Camping: ** Camping Arc en ciel, route de Goult (140 sites), Tel: (90) 05 67 17.

Medical Care: Physician, Tel: (90) 75 64 90.

Restaurants: ** La Tarasque, rue Richard Casteau, Tel: (90) 05 63 86, complete meals 155-227 FF.

** David, Place de la Poste, Tel: (90) 05 60 13, the restaurant has an excellent view of an ochre cliff, complete meals 100-280 FF.

** Val de Fées, Tel: (90) 05 64 99, complete meals 125-178 FF.

La Treille, rue du Four, Tel: (90) 05 64 47, complete meals from 88 FF.

Shopping: Wine, Soulard Joseph Domaine Ste Croix.

Sports Facilities: The riding stalls and hotel "Le trèfle à cinq feuilles, Edmond Freess "Les Madons," Tel: (90) 75 63 90, offers room and board; Haras de la Bergère, Pony-Club etc., Tel: (90) 75 63 77.

Important Addresses: Tourist Information: Place de la Poste, Tel: (90) 05 60 25.

Rustrel

Population: about 390; elevation: 432 metres (1,413 feet)

Rustrel is situated in a wooded area, 10 km (6¼ miles) northeast of Apt, accessible via the D 22. The main attraction are the ochre cliffs, called "Colorado of Rustrel," south of this small village. The red ochre rocks can be reached on foot and they are even more impressive than those in →*Roussillon.* The town hall is housed in a château from the 17th century.

Hotel: ** Auberge du Rustreou, 3 place de la Fête, Tel: (90) 74 24 12, 6 rooms 158-215 FF.
Camping: ** Camping le Colorado (200 sites, Tel: (90) 74 00 95.

Saignon

Population: about 690; altitude: 492 metres (1,609 feet)
The D 48 leads 4 km (2½ miles) southeast of Apt to the high-lying, once fortified mountain village of Saignon.

Saignon / **Sights**

The small Romanesque church from the 12th century was rebuilt and expanded in the 16th and 17th century. It has a beautifully carved wooden entry portal. The idyllic village square with the former washing area as its focus and the magnificent Fontaine de Sollier makes for a perfect place to linger. A steep path leads to a small chapel and the remains of the village fortifications and fortress complex. The preserved portions of the fortress have been very well

Over the roofs of Saignon, the small mountain village still has the remnants of an old fortress

restored; today, this is under private ownership. From the small plateau is a fantastic view of Apt and the Coulon Valley, the picturesque rooftops of Saignon all the way to Mont Ventoux. A few hundred yards east of Saignon lies the former Benedictine monastery of Abbaye Saint-Eusèbe from the 11th century. Today, only a church remains. During the 15th century, the monks abandoned the monastery and it then became private property.

Saignon / **Practical Information**

Accommodation: The "Auberge du Presbytère," Tel: (90) 74 11 50, offers accommodation.

Restaurants: The small restaurant "auberge du Presbytère" serves tasty snacks and inexpensive meals.

Shopping: In addition to the small village grocery stores, there is a sattlery (Sellerie) offering artistic and very tasteful work.

The expressive façades of St-Rémy-de-Provence

Saint-Didier

Halfway between Pernes-les-Fontaines and Vénasque on the D 28, one should make a short stop in Saint-Didier. Through a massive gateway, one will come to the magnificent Renaissance castle built from the 15th through 17th centuries. It was remodelled in 1862 and now serves as a psychiatric and neurological clinic.

St-Gilles →*Camargue*

St. Michel-de-Figolet (Monastery)

St. Michel-de-Figolet is located on the D 35 between Avignon and Tarascon.

St. Michel-de-Figolet / **History**

The history of this monastery dates back to the 10th century, when Benedictine monks from Montmajour founded a this monastery for ailing monks due to the beauty of the area and the purity of the air. Throughout history, the monastery became the possession of different orders of monks, and today it belongs to the Premonstratensian monks. The monastery is beautifully situated amid forests and thyme fields. This explains the name of this monastery, which can be traced back to the Proveçal word "ferigoulo," meaning thyme. As in the Middle Ages, the monastery remains a site of pilgrimage even today.

St. Michel-de-Figolet / **Sights**

The original chapel, Notre-Dame-du-Bon-Remède, now forms the side portion of the monastery church built in the 19th century. The interior of the church is painted in several colours (blue, red and gold) and has frescoes on the walls and ceilings. The adjacent cloister originates from the beginning of the 12th century, while construction on the monastery church St-Michel was begun in the 11th century. In the museum, chemists' vessels and equipment for distilling is on display, which the monks used earlier as well as today to make their famous liqueur.

St-Rémy-de-Provence

Population: about 8,400; elevation 60 m (196 feet)

St-Rémy-de-Provence is accessible via the N 571 and is located 21 km (13 miles) south of Avignon. St-Rémy-de-Provence is a small city with a great deal of flair. Taking place here is energetic commercial trade of seed for fruits and vegetables. The inner city is surrounded by a circular boulevard lined with plane tress.

St-Rémy-de-Provence / **History**

This city was originally founded by survivors from the nearby Gallo-Roman city of Glanum, which was destroyed in the 3rd century by Germanic tribes marching through the city. During the Middle Ages, this city was given the name Saint Rémy after Remigius, a saint who lived in the 6th century. Unfortunately, very little architecture remains from this period. The city did not become widely known for its buildings, with the exception of those at the excavation site of →*Glanum,* but more so for two personalities who resided here: first, the physician and astrologist Nostradamus, who was born here in 1503 and enjoys growing popularity today *(→Salon-de-Provence).* The second is the Dutch painter Vincent van Gogh, who lived here in 1889 for almost a year in Saint-Paul-de-Mausole sanatorium, which was formerly a monastery. During this time he produced 150 paintings. One of these, "The Irises," was auctioned off for $53.5 million (£30 million), on November 11, 1987, the highest price ever for a work of art.

St-Rémy-de-Provence / **Sights**

The Saint-Martin on Place de République is relatively "young." The church was built during the past century in classicist architecture on the ruins of its predecessor, which dated back to the 14th century. Only the bell tower of the original church has remained standing. In the centre of town, beautifully situated on a large square, is the lovely town hall, housed in what was formerly a monastery. The walk to the house where Nostradamus was born nearby on Rue Hoche, is not worth the effort: the house is dilapidated. More worthwhile is a visit to the Alpilles-Museum (Musée des Alpilles Pierre de Brun). This museum exhibits traditional folk art and keepsakes from Nostradamus. A taste of Glanum can be found in the Hôtel de Sade, which is located across from the museum. Housed in a stately building from the 15th and 16th centuries, one will be able to see the excavated finds such as tools, ceramics, tombs, sarcophagi and altars. An attraction outside the city is the former monastery Saint-Paul-de-Mausole, in which Vincent van Gogh spent the last part of his life from 1889 to 1890. Worth seeing are mainly the original parts of the building, dating back to the 12th century; the Romanesque bell tower; the cloisters; and the church, restored in the 19th century.

St-Rémy-de-Provence / **Practical Information**

Accommodation

Hotels: *** Host. du Vallon de Valrugues, chemin Canto Cigalo, Tel: (90) 92 04 40, 24 rooms 400-580 FF, complete meals 260-350 FF.

*** Château des Alpilles (without restaurant), 2 km (1¼ miles) non the D 31, Tel: (90) 92 03 33, attractive manor house from the 19th century, located in a park, 17 rooms 560-750 FF.
** Le Castelet des Alpilles, place Mireille, Tel: (90) 92 07 21, 20 rooms 95-370 FF, complete meals 100-200 FF.
** Soleil (without restaurant), avenue Pasteur, Tel: (90) 92 00 63, 15 rooms 200-260 FF.
* Arts, 30 boulevard Victor-Hugo, Tel: (90) 92 08 50, 17 rooms 120-220 FF, complete meals 68-150 FF.
Camping: Mas de Nicolas (north of town), avenue Théodore-Aubenal, Tel: (90) 92 27 05, 140 sites.
Montplaisir, chemin Montplaisir, Tel: (90) 92 22 70, 90 sites.
Automobile Repair: Citroën, Ford, Peugeot-Talbot, Renault.
Entertainment: In addition to a cinema, discotheque and nightclub, there are numerous concerts. More detailed information is available through the Office de Tourisme. During the tourist season, there are also Provençale bullfights.

A number of houses in the Provence are naturally decorated with a blanket of vines

Medical Care: There are eight physicians five dentist and numerous specialists as well as three pharmacies and two clinics in St-Rémy-de-Provence.

Restaurants: ** Jardin de Frédéric, 8 boulevard Gambetta, Tel: (90) 92 27 76, complete meals 110-180 FF.

Seven kilometres (4½ miles) outside of town via the D 5 in Maillane: ** Oustalet Maïanen, Tel: (90) 95 74 60, complete meals 100-150 FF.

Shopping: Wednesdays, a typically Provençal market in the old city, Saturdays a grocery market on the place de la Marie.

Sports Facilities: Swimming pool, route de Avignon; tennis quartier Sans-Souci; gliding centre Aéro-club de Romanin, route de Marseille, Tel: (90) 92 08 43; hiking, cycling and fishing (large lake) in the Alpilles; horseback riding: Club Hippique des Antiques, rue Etienne Astier, Tel: (90) 92 30 55; Mr. Lilamand, 10 chemin Croix des Vertus, Tel: (90) 92 19 62; Le Ranch, Mas Pellegrin, route d'Avignon, Tel: (90) 92 16 97.

Transportation: There are buses operating regularly to Avignon, Tarascon, Cavaillon, Salon-de-Provence, Aix-en-Provence and Marseille.

In June and July, the blooming lavender fields paint the landscape with vivid colour

Important Addresses: Office de Tourisme, pl. Jean-Jaurès, Tel: (90) 92 05 22.
Town Hall: Tel: (90) 92 08 10.
Gendarmerie/Police: Tel: (90) 92 00 47.
Taxi: on place de République, Tel: (90) 92 12 37, (90) 92 10 82, (90) 92 09 71.

St-Saturnin-d'Apt

Population: approximately 1200; elevation: 400 metres (1,308 feet)
About 9 km (5½ miles) north of Apt is the small village of St-Saturnin-d'Apt, overshadowed by the ruins of an old fortress and a Romanesque chapel.

St-Saturnin-d'Apt / **Practical Information**

Accommodation:
Hotel: ** Les Voyageurs, place Gambetta, Tel: (90) 75 42 08, 14 rooms 96-210 FF, complete meals from 90 FF.
Camping: ** Des Chênes Blancs, route de Gargas (D 101), Tel: (90) 74 09 20, 600 sites, swimming pool.
Restaurants: ** St-Hubert (with 8 rooms 74 154 FF), place de la Fraternité, Tel: (90) 75 42 02, complete meals 120-180 FF.

Salon-de-Provence

Population: 35,500; elevation: 82 metres (268 feet)
Salon-de-Provence is situated halfway between Arles and Aix-en-Provence. Since 1936, it has been home to the flight training school of the French Air Force.

Salon-de-Provence / **History**

Salon was already an important transportation hub during the Roman times. Located on the Via Aurelia which ran from Italy to Nîmes, this favourable location helped the town to become an economically significant centre during the Middle Ages. In the year 1032, Salon fell to the German Emperor. Subject to the emperor alone, Charles IV granted the city of Salon certain privileges. Previously, the city was known as a centre for agriculture but today, the petrochemical industry is also an important branch of the economy.

Salon-de-Provence / **Sights**

The city offers good parking. In addition to a parking area on Place Général-de-Gaulle, there is also a parking garage. There is a moss-covered fountain on the Place Crousillat (located on the boulevards which surround the old city) from the 18th century. The old city is best entered through one of the two city gates, one of which, the Porte Bourg-Neuf, is from the 13th century. The other, the Porte de l'Horloge with its wrought-iron bell tower, dates back to the 17th century. Also directly on the Rue de l'Horloge is the St. Michael's Church from the 13th century. The church has a magnificent front entrance and to the rear, its bell wall embellished with five rounded arches. The way leads further along by buildings from the 17th and 18th century to the city's castle, perched high above the city. The castle is called Château de l'Empéri, reminiscent of when the Provence came under the rule of the Holy Roman Empire in 1032. The complex has two courtyards and a total length of 170 metres (556 feet). It was built under the direction of the Bishops of Arles in the 10th century. Originally, it served in the defence of the city; however, in the 12th and 13th centuries it was expanded and modified, taking on the character of a castle. The earthquake of 1909 destroyed portions of the castle and the surrounding village. Today, the palace houses a military museum which displays weaponry, uniforms and other military collections. Not far from the castle complex is the residential house of Nostradamus, the famous son of this city. This well-known physician and astrologist (born in St-Rémy in 1503) lived here from 1549 until his death in 1566. In addition to his activities as a scientist, he worked on prophecies and predictions, some of which have indeed been confirmed. This makes his residence which has been converted into a museum an attraction not only for the astrologically inclined. To the north of the old city lies the Laurentius Church from the 14th century, impressive through its spacious interior. Here, in one of the side chapels is the grave of Nostradamus.

Salon-de-Provence / **Practical Information**

Accommodation

Hotels: ** Midi (without restaurant), 518 allées de Craponne, Tel: (90) 53 34 67, 27 rooms 150-250 FF.

** Roi René (without restaurant), 561 allées de Craponne, Tel: (90) 53 20 22, 30 rooms 160-250 FF.

** Vendôme, (without restaurant), 34 rue Marécal-Joffre, Tel: (90) 56 01 96, 23 rooms 135-150 FF.

* Sélect-H. (without restaurant), 35 rue Suffren, Tel: (90) 56 07 17, 19 rooms 130-140 FF.

Camping: Nostradamus (5 km/3miles north of Salon), Tel: (90) 56 08 36, 83 sites.

Automobile Repair: Alfa-Romeo, Ford, Honda, Peugeot, Renault.

Restaurants: *** Robin, 1 boulevard Georges-Clémenceau, Tel: (90) 56 06 53, serving specialities, complete meals 230-310 FF.
** Le Touring, 20 place Crousillat, Tel: (90) 56 00 07, complete meals 75-170 FF.
** Craponne, 146 allées de Craponne, Tel: (90) 53 23 92, meals 71-145 FF.
* Le Poêlon, 71 allées de Craponne, Tel: (90) 53 31 38, meals 99-160 FF.
Sports Facilities: Golf course de l'École de l'Air, Tel: (90) 53 90 90.
Important Addresses: Office de Tourisme and Automobile Club, 56 cours Gimon, Tel: (90) 56 27 60.

Santon

The name Santon comes from the Provençale word santoùn (minor saint). Jean-Luis Lagnel (1764-1822) was the first to have the idea to produce inexpensive, colourfully painted nativity scenes from clay. Today, from these small beginnings, an industry has developed for the mass production of these amiable figures. Numerous would-be artists have flocked to this branch of production and it is important when purchasing such figures to not only look for originality but also for quality. Originally, these statuettes were portrayals of Provençale characters from the great nativity scene (la grande crèche) which represented the common folk, for example the market woman, the scissor-grinder, the vintner and the shepherd. Many churches display the beautiful nativity scenes with the Santon figures during the entire year. Many of these nativity scenes tour the country, making it important to note the signs for 'grande crèche.' Such a nativity scene can cover an area of up to 15 square metres (162 square feet) and contain moving figures which represent village life in its entirety.

Sault

Population: about 1,200; elevation: 780 metres (2,551 feet)
The once Roman city of Saltus lies 32 km (20 miles) north of Apt. Sault makes a good starting point for excursions to Mont Ventoux, and Gorges de la Nesque *(→Nesque Canyon)* as well as to the Haute Provence. Upon arrival, one sees only few villages; now and then, there are self-sufficient farms in a wooded and mountainous landscape with extensive lavender fields. Sault is famous for its honey and lavender. The lavender distilleries are an indication of the importance of this economic branch.

Sault / **Sights**

As in many other villages, the church makes up the focus of Sault. It is an impressively simple and congenially unadorned church from the 12th century.

At the front of the church, next to the altar is a Borie. Upon closer inspection, the purpose will become clear: during the Christmas season, this Borie is where the nativity scene with Santon figures is set up *(→Bories, Santon).* In addition, there is a small archaeological and geological museum with a large library.

Sault / **Practical Information**

Accommodation

Hotels: ** Deffends, route de Saint-Trinit, Tel: (90) 64 01 41, 10 rooms 280 FF, complete meals 130-180 FF.

* Albion (without restaurant), avenue Oratoire, Tel: (90) 64 06 22, modern accommodation, 10 rooms 210-230 FF.

* Relais du Ventoux (5 km/3 miles via the D 942 in Aurel), Tel: (90) 64 00 62, 14 rooms 110-160 FF, complete meals 60-110 FF.

Camping: ** Camping Municipal du Deffends, route de Saint-Trinit (300 sites), Tel: (90) 64 02 30.

Automobile Repair: Renault Garage de la Lavande, Tel: (90) 64 02 41.

Medical Care: There are two physicians, a dentist and a pharmacy in Sault. Hospital: rue de l'Hôpital, Tel: (90) 64 00 32.

Shopping: On Wednesdays, there is a market; excellent lavender honey; nougat; goat's cheese.

Sports Facilities: Tennis, horseback riding hotel/excursions: Auberge du Bourguignon, Tel: (90) 64 01 02.

Transportation: There are buses to Apt and Carpentras. Taxi, Tel: (90) 64 02 17 and (90) 64 01 35.

Important Addresses

Tourist Information: avenue de la Promenade, Tel: (90) 64 01 21.

Town Hall: place du Marché, Tel: (90) 64 02 30.

Post Office: avenue de la Promenade, Tel: (90) 64 02 00.

Gendarmerie/Police: quartier Roumane, Tel: (90) 64 00 04.

Sénanque (Monastery)

From Gordes heading north on the D 177 through a rocky countryside with only sparse vegetation, the road is narrow and can only accommodate two-way traffic at a few stretches. in this relatively barren landscape, the Cistercian monks founded the expansive Sénanque monastery in 1148. The location of the monastery is unparalleled in terms of beauty: especially in summer, the lightly coloured building makes an impressive contrast to the blooming lavender fields in the foreground. The name Sénanque can be traced back

to the river which flows through this valley: the Senanole (Sana Aqua = healthy water or Sine Aqua = without water; this, because the riverbed is often dried up). Up until 1969, monks lived in this monastery. Today, the monastery has been adapted to the numerous visitors. The unembellished rooms of the monastery can all be toured and there are often concerts in the monastery with its fantastic acoustics. One especially attractive aspect of the monastery is the cloister with its columns — no one column is the same as any other. The life of the Cistercians becomes clear from a tour of the monastery: they worked hard and diligently and had to do without a great deal. Only one room was heated and the monks were only allowed to speak with one another in the cloister. In the adjacent buildings, is an exhibition on the Sahara with photos and various articles from the live of a Tuareg tribe.
Shopping: For music lovers, there is a sales room with a good selection of record of sacred music and chorales. The selection of literature ranges from spiritual works and world literature to travel guides for the Provence and children's books. Locally produced products like Eau de Lavande and honey are relatively expensive, but do have the "Sénanque seal." Tel: (90) 72 02 05.

Silvacane (Monastery)

Accessible from Cadenet via the D 561 is the former monastery Silvacane. Along with Sénanque, this counts among the most significant Cistercian monasteries in the Provence. Built in 1144, it witnessed a time of prosperity up until its destruction in 1357. Now owned by the French government, this complex includes a church with a noteworthy portal. The cloister is spanned by Romanesque arches.

Simiane-la-Rotonde

Population 400; elevation: 630-900 metres (2,060-2,943 feet)
The small town of Simiane-la-Rotonde is 25 kilometres northeast of Apt on the D 22 and D 51. The trip through the beautiful landscape leads past the ochre cliffs of Rustrel and along the first Force de Frappe military complex (Sault is not far from here).

Simiane-la-Rotonde / **Sights**

The old upper portion of this picturesque village is not accessible by car. This village has remained relatively untouched by tourism and offers a quaint atmosphere with countless flowerpots and exquisitely carved wooden doors. To reach the ruins of the castle with its rotonde, one must climb the steep streets and stairways. This castle was once the residence of the Lords of Simiane, who were once the most significant noble family in Vaucluse. From here, there is a beautiful view of the plain.

Speed Limits

In towns and cities, the speed limit is 60 km/h; on roads outside of the city limits, driving 90 km/h is allowed (only 80 km/h when raining). On the motorways the speed limit is 130 km/h (when raining, 110 km/h). Those who have only recently gotten their driver's licence are generally only allowed to drive at most 90 km/h during the first year.

Sports

Cycling: The tourist information office will be able to provide cyclists with pre-planned cycle tours, categorised by level of difficulty. Especially beautiful tours are through the →*Alpilles.* Bicycles can be rented in a number of towns.
Fishing: There are numerous opportunities to fish in the Provence, be it in the lakes, rivers or streams.
Hiking: The hiking areas are well marked, especially in the Luberon and Alpilles regions. The appropriate hiking maps are available from the tourist information offices. During the summer, many areas close due to fire hazard.
Horseback Riding: The Provence is ideal for horseback riding and there are also an according number of opportunities.
Hunting: Hunting is especially popular in the Provence and one can often hear rifle shots in the forests. One does, however, require a hunting permit from the local police department.
Mountain Climbing: Cliffs and mountains with ideal conditions await the mountain climber in the Provence.
Skiing: Excellent winter sport conditions can be found in the French Alps. In addition, there are also some attractive winter sport resorts near Mont Ventoux.
Swimming: Meanwhile, many of the hotels and camping areas have swimming pools in addition to the numerous municipal pools. One can also go to the nearby Côte d'Azur.
Tennis: Most hotels and camping areas will be equipped with tennis courts.

Stes-Maries-de-la-Mer →*Camargue*

Tarascon

Population: 11,000; elevation: 17 metres (56 feet)
Tarascon is located approximately 23 kilometres (14¼ miles) from Avignon on the left bank of the Rhône.

Tarascon / **History**

The Celtic-Ligurian settlement of Tarusco on the island of Jovarnica in the Rhône River was already a centre for trade and commerce for the Greek city of Massalia (Marseille) before the Roman times. Shipping on the Rhône was secured through the construction of the Roman Castrum during the middle of the 1st century A.D. The settlement was then connected with Beaucaire on the opposite banks of the river by a bridge and the settlement developed into an important commercial harbour. Tarascon experienced a golden age during the 15th century under the rule of the art lover King René. He surrounded himself with poets and singers in the castle on the banks of the river which he had expanded. Today, Tarascon is an important hub for the transportation of fruits and vegetables produced in the hinterland.

Tarascon / **Sights**

Tarascon became famous through "Tartarin of Tarascon" the title figure in the novel by Alphonse Daudet (1840-1897). This charlatan made fun of the passion of the hunt, which was often only a pretence for men to get together among themselves. For the reader who is definitely convinced that Tartarin really did once live, the search for his house will not be futile — this since October 1985: the house has been reproduced true to the fictive character with attention to details, making fiction into reality. The garden is especially deserving of an attentive stroll: a common green lily is marked with a sign with an exquisite name à la Tartarin. Inside the house, his living room, music room and bedroom are furnished with painstaking attention to detail. In the Sainte-Marthe Church from the 12th to 15th century is the sarcophagus of Saint Martha, located in the crypt. The southern portal of this church is Romanesque. According to a legend, the city was freed from the cannibalistic monster Tarasque by Saint Martha who came from Stes-Maries-de-la-Mer. In honour of this event, the city of Tarascon celebrates the Tarasque festival every year on the last Sunday in June. The château on the banks of the Rhône was most likely built where the Roman Castrum once stood in the 12th century and was then expanded by King René in the 15th century. The height of this massive, almost windowless fortress is fifteen stories. The interior of the complex is characterised by a number of unfurnished halls grouped around an inner courtyard. One should also not miss a stroll through the Rue des Halles.

Tarascon / **Practical Information**

Accommodation

Hotels: ** Provence (without restaurant), 7 boulevard Victor-Hugo, Tel: (90) 91 06 43, 11 rooms 260-300 FF.

* St-Jean, 24 boulevard Victor-Hugo, Tel: (90) 91 13 87, 12 rooms from 165 FF.

* Terminus, place Colonel-Berrurier, Tel: (90) 91 18 95, 22 rooms 80-120 FF, complete meals from 50 FF.

Camping: Tartarin, route de Vallabrègues, on the banks of the Rhône near the castle, Tel: (90) 91 01 46, 90 sites.

St-Gabriel (southeast of Tarascon), Tel: (90) 91 19 83, 50 sites.

Youth Hostel: (55 beds), 31 boulevard Gambetta, Tel: (90) 91 04 08.

Automobile Repair: Citroën, Renault.

Medical Care: Hospital: route d'Arles, Tel: (90) 91 04 54.

Shopping: Market on Tuesdays; city where the Soleiado fabrics are produced; for the sweet-tooth: Tartarinades (pralines filled with liqueur).

Transportation: Buses operate to Avignon, Nîmes, Arles, St-Rémy and Cavaillon — information is available in the tourist information office.

Important Addresses: Office de Tourisme, 59 rue Halles, Tel: (90) 91 03 52.

Telephone

The international country code for France is 33 (from the US 011 33; from the UK 010 33). To reach the UK from France, dial 19, wait for the dial tone and then dial 44 followed by the UK area code leaving out the initial 0 and then the local number. To call the US dial 19, wait for the dial tone and then dial 1 followed by the area code and the number. Most public telephones are equipped for international calls. The pay telephones will accept 20 Centimes, ½ Franc, 1 Franc and 5 Franc. Most pay telephones accept only telephone cards which can be purchased at all post offices for 40 FF or 120 FF.

Le Thor

Population: 5,000; elevation: 70 metres (229 feet)

Located on the N 100 about 23 kilometres (15 miles) east of Avignon near Isle-sur-la-Sorgue is the town of Le Thor, in the fruit and vegetable producing region.

Le Thor / **Sights**

The remains of the city fortifications, a bridge and a tower from the Middle Ages as well as a Romanesque church from the 12th century with external pillars forming a four sided apsis are among the attractions of this city. Located nearby is the grotto →*Thouzon.*

Le Thor / **Practical Information**

Accommodation: Camping Lejantou, Tel: (90) 33 90 07, 300 sites.

Restaurant: Restaurant le Tilt, 14 cours Gambetta, Tel: (90) 33 80 23, complete meals from 65 FF.

Shopping: Market on Saturdays; Wine Coopérative

Transportation: S.N.C.F. Train Station.

Important Addresses

Office de Tourisme: Place du Marché.

Post Office: Place du Marché.

Taxi and Ambulance: chemin des Estourants, Tel: (90) 33 97 36.

Thouzon Cave

About 2.5 kilometres (1½ miles) north of Le Thor on the D 16 one will come upon the "Grottes de Thouzon," a massive cavern with stalactites and stalagmites, discovered in 1902. The cavern is open from Palm Sunday to October 31, daily from 9 am to 7 pm; during the winter, on Sunday afternoons from 2 to 8 pm.

Time of Day

France is on Middle European Time, one hour later than the UK and 6 (New York) to 9 (Los Angeles) hours later than the US.

Tipping

Most hotel and restaurant bills will include "servis compris" (service included). Despite this, it is customary to round the sum of the bill up to the next 5 FF. This is more than a small gratuity because service personnel are paid very poorly.

Tourist Information

In almost all of the larger cities, a sign with an "i" indicates the direction of the Tourist Information Offices (Bureau de Tourisme, Office de Tourisme or Syndicat d'Initiative). There one can obtain all of the necessary information like maps, brochures about sights, about sports facilities, campgrounds, special events, and hotel and restaurant registries, or even information on holiday apartments. At some of the Tourist Information Offices it is also possible to book hotel rooms. Tickets for special events and public transportation are also usually available through the Tourist Information Offices.

Important Addresses:

French Tourist Information Bureau for the Département of Var: Office de Tourisme, 8 Avenue Colbert, F-83000 Toulon, Tel: (94) 22 08 22.

For the Department of Bouches-du-Rhône: Office de Tourisme, 4 Canebière, F-13000 Marseille, Tel: (91) 54 91 11.

For the Département of Vaucluse: Office de Tourisme, 41 Cours Jean-Jaurès, F-84000 Avignon, Tel: (90) 82 65 11.

Traffic Regulations

If not otherwise designated by traffic signs then the person to the right at an intersection has the right of way. In lighted streets it is permitted to drive at night using only parking lights.

Seat belts must be worn throughout France.

The blood alcohol limit is 0.8 per mill.

The French police are very strict and the fines are quite high. No exceptions are made for foreigners. If caught driving under the influence of alcohol, the penalty can be a very high fine in addition to losing ones licence and can be as extreme as imprisonment or even confiscation of the automobile.

Travel Documents

Visitors to France need valid identification in the form of an identity card (for members of the EC) or a passport. Children under 16 years of age must have a children's identity card or must be entered in the parents' passport. Drivers must have a valid driver's licence and the automobile registration. In addition, it is advisable to also have the international insurance card handy. A nationality sticker must also be affixed to the rear of the car.

Travel in the Provence

The French network of rural roads are good to very good and what at first sight might appear to be a rather chaotic driving style, prove in fact to be quite considerate. Without a car, travel options are much more limited: a bicycle offers a good opportunity to explore the countryside more intensely; however, because of the large differences in altitude from one town to the next, it can get quite

strenuous. Complicating this is the fact that the roadways are not equipped with separate bicycle lanes, making this somewhat dangerous.
Those who chose to use public transportation must plan a good deal of time and patience into their travel itinerary. The bus and rail connections throughout the Provence are quite poor. There are hardly any local train routes in the Provence, but there are bus routes beginning at the train stations, making it possible to continue the journey to a number of destinations. Buses do operate to smaller villages; however, they do not operate very often. Tickets can be bought aboard the buses as well as at the ticket counters, in the tobacco shops and at kiosks. Transportation schedules and routes are available in the tourist information offices.
The relative inconvenience of the public transportation in the Provence is one explanation why the French prefer to drive. Without a car, it might not be feasible to see all one would like within the time one has available. This might make renting a car a worthwhile option. *(→Car Rental)*

Travelling to the Provence

By Car: Generally speaking, there are two routes to reach the Provence when travelling by car: those who would like to see as much as possible along the way and also have ample time should use the country roads. In spite of the toll (about £7/$12) the motorway from Lyon can be recommended since the Rhône Valley has been developed into an industrial area. For those who would like to arrive quickly, the motorway network is recommended. The motorway tolls will total around £20/$40.
By Train: If one is less excited about driving all the way to the Provence, then one should check into rail travel where it is possible to transport an automobile as well. The main rail hubs are Avignon and Marseille. One option is to make a slight detour to Paris. From Paris, one can travel with one of the fastest trains in the world through the Rhône Valley to Marseille.
By Coach: Because more and more people are discovering the Provence, many travel agencies offer complete coach tour packages. This form of travel is, however, restricted by set schedules, routes and sights.
The beauty and true character of the Provence in the rural area off the beaten track will of course be missed when travelling by coach. One should inquire at local travel agencies about coach tours offering a high level of flexibility for individual excursions.
By Air: Numerous flights are available to Marseille. Within France, Air France offers connecting flights to Nîmes.

By Ship: For those travelling from another Mediterranean country, it is also possible to reach the Provence by ship. Marseille is a large international harbour where numerous international ship lines dock.

Vaison-la-Romaine

Population: 5,800; elevation: 200 metres (654 feet)
The most Roman of all the cities in the Provence, Vaison-la-Romaine, is located about 28 kilometres (17½ miles) north of Carpentras on the D 938 on the Ouvèze River. The entire city is an over 2,000 year old museum with an abundance of archaeological excavations.

Vaison-la-Romaine / **History**

The first inhabitants of this area were the Ligurians, who were followed by the Vocontier, a Celtic tribe which established their central settlement here. The Romans first conquered the city in the year 118 A.D. and built the city of Vasio Vocontiorum into one of the most significant cities in their province of Gallia Narbonensis. At the end of the 3rd century, the city was Christianised and the bishops which followed became so powerful that with the fall of the Roman Empire (500 A.D.) they took over the rule of the city. In 1160, the Count of Toulouse took control of the city and had a castle and an new upper city built on the opposite banks of the Ouvèze River. Most of the residents move to this protected portion of the city. The abandoned lower city fell into decay during the course of the centuries until a repopulation of this area occurred in the 18th century. Buildings were constructed using the rubble from the old Roman city. The excavations, which began in 1907, still uncover many new finds from the Roman period.

Vaison-la-Romaine / **Sights**

When approaching this city from Orange, at the entrance to the city, one will see the Notre-Dame Church founded in the 6th century and reconstructed in the 12th century. The marble altar inside the church is very interesting as are the graves of the bishops along the walls. A small religious museum is located in the cloister (11th century). Along the Avenue Jules Ferry, one will come upon the first larger excavation site, the "Quartier de la Villasse" with a street lined with shops and a house named after one of the archaeological finds, the "House of the Silver Bust." The impressive excavation complex has several halls, inner courtyards and a garden. The second building, "the House of the Dolphin," has a beautiful atrium. More rich in archaeological finds and larger as well is the excavation in the second Roman district on Rue B.-Noël in the Quartier de Puymin. In addition to the ruins of Roman rental housing, one will find an exemplary patrician house: the House of Messii. Adjacent to it, one can visit the courtyard of Pompeius with its columns. As a highlight to the visit, one can see the Roman theatre with a diameter of 96 metres (461 feet) and an intact gallery of columns. The theatre is adroitly built on and into the slopes. Across the Roman bridge built of stone and still intact today, one can visit the Haute Ville (upper city) now inhabited once more. Worth seeing in this area are the ruins of the medieval castle.

Vaison-la-Romaine / **Practical Information**

Accommodation

Hotels: ** Le Beffroi, Haute Ville, rue de l'Evêché, Tel: (90) 36 04 71, a lovely estate from the 16th century, 21 rooms 220-460 FF, complete meals 98-185 FF.

* Burrhus, 2 place Montfort, Tel: (90) 36 00 11, 14 rooms 220-300 FF, complete meals from 95 FF.

* Théâtre Romain, place du 11 novembre, Tel: (90) 36 05 87, 21 rooms 75-170 FF.

Camping: Le Moulin de César, Tel: (90) 36 00 78, 1000 sites.

Automobile Repair: Citroën, Fiat, Opel-GM, Peugeot, Renault, Talbot.

Restaurants: * Le Bateleur, place Th.-Aubanel, Tel: (90) 36 28 04, complete meals 94-125 FF.

9.5 kilometres away in Séguret via the D 88: *** La Table du Comtat (Gomez), Tel: (90) 46 91 49, excellent specialities, reservations are recommended, complete meals 195-370 FF, also offering 8 rooms for 350-600 FF.

Shopping: Market on Tuesdays; wine: Cave Coopérative.

Sports Facilities: Riding Hotel Les Estaillades — Sainte-Croix, Tel: (90) 36 22 09, swimming pool.

Important Addresses: Office de Tourisme, Place du Chanoine Sautel, Tel: (90) 36 02 11.

Valréas

Population: 8,500; elevation: 250 metres (817.5 feet)

Valréas is located 30 kilometres north of Vaison-la-Romaine on the D 941 in the Coronne Valley.

Valréas / **Sights**

In addition to the old, ornamented houses of nobility, the Notre-Dame de Nazareth Church from the 11th and 15th century is worth seeing with its organ and the Chapelle des Pénitents Blancs both from the 16th century. The town hall is located in the Château de Simiane from the 15th century and renovated around 1700. Today it is an architectural monument. A special event takes place here annually on the 23rd of June: the Fête du petit St. Jean, a festival with over 500 years of tradition. A boy between 3 and 5 years of age is chosen as the petit Saint Jean, symbolising the patron saint of the city, Saint Martin. The child is then carried through the city on a sedan chair by torchlight in a mirthful procession. During the year to follow, the city and the fertility of the fields are under his protection.

Valréas / **Practical Information**

Accommodation

** Gd Hôtel, 28 avenue Général-de-Gaulle, Tel: (90) 35 00 26, 18 rooms 170-300 FF, complete meals 75-160 FF.

Automobile Repair: Citroën.

Entertainment: For over 500 years, the festival in honour of the minor St. Jean has been celebrated on June 23.

Shopping: The market takes place on Wednesdays.

Important Addresses: Office de Tourisme, Place Aristide-Briand, Tel: (90) 35 04 71.

Vauvenargues

Population: 450; elevation: 411 metres (1,344 feet)

Located 14 kilometres (9 miles) east of Aix-en-Provence on the D 10 is the town of pilgrimage for Picasso fans. Pablo Picasso (1881-1973) bought the castle here from the 17th century at the edge of the village in 1958. The castle was built on the ruins of a fortress from the 14th century. Picasso is buried in the castle gardens. The castle is not open to the public. It was home to his widow up until her suicide in 1986. Vauvenargues is an idyllic town and from the castle, one will have a fantastic view of the Sainte-Victoire above the city.

Hotel: * Le Moulin de Provence, Tel: (42) 66 02 22, 12 rooms 95-160 FF, complete meals from 95 FF.

Vegetation

The landscapes of the Provence are, on the one hand, quite Mediterranean, and on the other, rugged and barren. Mild winters and hot summers provide a favourable climate for plants sensitive to cold temperatures. The countryside is filled with herbs and their characteristic fragrances. The well known herbs

like rosemary, thyme and sage grow like weeds in the Provence and are among the basic herbs used in the regional cuisine *(→Spices).* In July, the famous lavender fields are in bloom. These flowers are harvested and used for manufacturing perfume in Grasse, among other regions. 85% of the lavender oil produced worldwide comes from the Provence. Small sachets filled with lavender blossoms, lavender water and soaps make nice souvenirs. In addition to the wilderness with its pine, cypress and the typical oak forests, there are large cultivated areas. Important agricultural produce includes melons, strawberries, asparagus, cabbage, tomatoes, grains and rice in the Camargue region. In addition to plantations producing cherries, almonds, peaches, pears and apricots, there are also olive trees originally imported from Greece. Olive trees are sensitive to frost, endangering their growth during the sometimes harsh winters. Longer periods of ground frost can destroy all of the olive trees in the region, and it takes up to 20 years before an olive tree will bear fruit. One will also see figs growing in the Provence, either on plantations or growing in the wild. Growing in private gardens, one will encounter the mulberry bush, typical for the Provence. These plants were imported in the 15th century by King René for the breeding of silkworms.
Grapes ripen in extensive vineyards and are processed into the popular rosé or red wines. The agricultural product that commands one of the highest prices on the market is less readily visible — the truffles *(→Cuisine).*

Vénasque

Population: 600; elevation: 310 metres (1,014 feet)
This very old and charming mountain village is about 11 kilometres (7 miles) southeast of Carpentras on the D 4. It is bordered on three sides by steep cliffs.

Vénasque / **Sights**

As a result of its location, the village of Vénasque is very narrow. Therefore, it is a good idea to park one's car at the parking area next to the Notre-Dame Church at the entrance to the village. Nest to this church from the 12th and 13th century (repeatedly reconstructed) is the Baptisterium. This is said to have been built in the 6th century, making it one of the oldest religious architectural monuments in France. What remains unclear to date is whether or not it is actually a Baptistère (baptismal chapel) or a memorial chapel in honour of the martyrs. Vénasque was at one point in time the residence of the bishop and remnants of the city fortifications can still be seen.

A special type of excursion is a drive east of Vénasque on the D 4 heading toward Murs and Apt: through the dense Forêt de Vénasque (the forest of Vénasque) the road winds through a picturesque landscape up to a mountain pass (Col de Murs).

Vénasque / **Practical Information**

Accommodation: *Hotel/Restaurant:* Les Ramparts, terrace with a beautiful view, Tel: (90) 66 02 79 and (90) 66 03 04, five rooms from 130 FF, complete meals from 70 FF.
Medical Care: In Vénasque, there is a physician, a dentist in the nearby town of Malemort and a pharmacy in Saint Didier.
Restaurant: ** Auberge de la Fontaine with 5 apartments at 590 FF, Tel: (90) 66 02 96, complete meals from 160 FF.
Shopping: Some shops offer tastefully crafted pottery and other handicrafts.
Sports Facilities: Tennis; horseback riding at the hotel Auberge de Saint Gens, Mme Frances, Tel: (90) 66 00 25, southwest of town in Le Beaucet.
Important Addresses: Tourist Information is available through the town hall (Marie), Tel: (90) 66 11 66.

Mont Ventoux

The shining summit of this 1,912 metre (6,252 foot) high landmark of the Provence can be seen from quite a distance. The peak seems to be covered with snow during the entire year — but this impression is deceptive. The mountain is wooded up to an altitude of 1,600 metres (5,280 feet), the summit is composed of light coloured limestone, making it impossible to see the snow melt in April and May. Petrarca first climbed the mountain in 1336 — for that time, an extraordinary achievement and also seemingly insane. Today, one can comfortably drive to the summit, where there is a breathtaking panorama. It is best to visit the summit during the early morning hours or in the evening. During the day, the weather is often hazy. At the summit, there is a weather station and an observatory. One should remember to wear warm clothing since a stiff breeze can make it quite chilly even during the height of summer.
Sports Facilities: Station du Mt-Serein (7 Téléskis/ski lifts).

Votive Pictures

When visiting the churches of the Provence, one cannot help but notice the vividly colourful and primitively painted votive pictures and the votive plaques. This is a type of folk art in connection with pilgrimages during the late Middle

Ages (votivus = Latin for "blessed by taking an oath"). Seeking help or solace in the midst of such fates as disease, misfortune or death, people often would take oaths. As a reminder of these vows, they had pictures painted, depicting the sought after grace. The picture would include the inscription "ex voto" (based on the vow). The simple and more common form is the votive plaque, which usually includes only the year and the phrase "was of help."

Wildlife

With the exception of the bulls and horses of the Camargue region, the Provence has few large wild animals. Visitors will find a wealth of birds and insects. Especially in the more mountainous regions, one will come across numerous species of lizards. Snakes are also very common, but hardly ever seen because they are very shy animals. The non-poisonous adder snakes are the most common, but there are a few poisonous vipers, making it a good idea to wear stable shoes and long trousers when hiking. This is also a good idea because of the scorpions. Most of the scorpions are harmless; however, even their stings can have unpleasant consequences. The typical "music" of the Provence is the song of the cicadas. Near ponds, streams, rivers and fish ponds, one will find another form of wildlife: the frogs, which are especially prevalent during twilight. What has meanwhile become a legend is the wild boar. It is possible that there might once more be wild boars in the Luberon Mountains now that this region has been made into a nature reserve.

Wine

About 60% of the wine produced in the Provence is rosé, some of which have a very good reputation with wine connoisseurs. Just to name a few: the fruity Bandol, the elegant Tavel and the Lirac — the last two, produced in the Avignon region — the hearty Côtes du Luberon and Côtes du Ventoux and the red wines from Châteauneuf-du-Pape. It is best to stop at one of the many wine coopératives to taste the various types available. When purchasing bottled wine one should take note of the quality designations on the bottle: the bottles marked A.O.C. or V.D.O.S. are first-class wines. However, many of the land wines will be surprisingly high in quality.

Youth Hostels

There are youth hostels in the cities of Aix-en-Provence, Fontaine-de-Vaucluse, Marseille, Nîmes, Les Stes-Maries-de-la-Mer and Tarascon. One must have an international youth hostel identity card.